Pagan Baby Names & Naming Rituals

By

Delilah Penn

Table of Contents:

Naming Rituals..……...3
Names (listed alphabetically with meaning)...........16
Names (listed by meaning).............................137
Bibliography....................…...................…......158

Naming Rituals

These rituals can be modified to be as formal or casual as you need. If done with a coven or a group of like-minded friends, the ritual you choose can be incorporated into an esbat or other circle. If those attending will include friends of other faiths, the rituals can be done without formally casting a circle, as a simple celebration of the child's birth.

Feel free to add or delete sections, or modify these rituals to make them more personal. (Adding the names of your preferred deities, etc.) They are just suggestions & ideas to get you started. Parts that are assigned to a High Priest or Priestess can be divided however you choose, and can even be split up among the members of the circle if you wish, to include as many as possible.

Stone's Energy Welcoming Ritual

Parent(s) & child move to the center of the circle. Each person in the circle then takes a turn presenting the child with their stone, which is chosen for its property or properties:

Celebrant steps forward & hold the stone out to child & parents:

I offer this gift of (stone) in hopes that the (property) it holds/represents will surround this child throughout his/her life.

Example:

I offer this gift of garnet in hopes that the strength it holds will surround this child throughout her life.

Parent:

We thank you for this gift.

The celebrant then lays the stone on the ground before parents & child. As the ritual continues, the stones should be laid in a circle so that the child is surrounded by their energy. Once all the stones have been presented, the celebrants should each focus their power on "their" offering as they all chant together"

"Lord & Lady we humbly ask

These stones to carry out their task.

Protect this child with their energy
As we will, so mote it be."

One person, or a couple if the gathering is large, then gathers the stones & places them in a basket or bag for the parents to carry home.

The stones should be kept in the nursery to keep their energy close to the child. An excellent way to do this is to place them in a small tabletop fountain within the room. The sound of the running water will soothe the child & will also keep the energy of the stones active through its constant motion.

Here are a few stones & their properties to get you started:

Agate: strength, courage, longevity, love

Amber: luck, healing, strength, protection

Hematite: grounding

Tiger's Eye: wealth, courage, luck

(This ritual can also be done using herbs instead of stones. Each offered herb can be placed in a basket in front of the child & parents, or placed around them in a circle. After the ceremony, the herbs can be sewn into a sachet to be kept in the child's room.)

Parents' Vows

Child is placed in a crib or seat of some sort, or can be held by the parents. Each parent takes a turn stepping forward & speaking:

Parents (To celebrants):

(Child's name) is a blessing from the Lord & Lady

And I am honored that she has bestowed this blessing upon me.

(To child):

I vow to guide as best I may

Through words & by my actions

To listen well & lend you strength

Through all of life's distractions.

(This can also be used for grandparents, or God(des) parents by changing the first part to:

(Child's name) is a blessing from the Lord & Lady

And I am honored that you offer

To share this blessing with me.)

Presentation to the Goddess

High Priestess calls the parents forward. They come forth with the child.

HPS: (Arms raised overhead, toward the moon if the ceremony is outdoors.)
> Goddess, (parents' names) come before you
> To present their child
> And to ask that you watch over him/her.

> (To parents) What name have you given him/her?

Parents: Lady, we present to you our child, (child's name).
> May she/he grow hale & hearty
> Under the watch of the Goddess.

Parents turn so that those gathered may see the child.

HPS: (To those gathered)
> Let us all greet (child's name) as our brother/sister.

All: Merry meet!

HPS: Let us all remember that, as (child) grows

He/she will see our actions as examples.
Let us all be worthy examples to (child)
And to all we meet.

All: So be it!

HPS: (to parents) Blessings to you and to (child).

(arms raised overhead once again)
Lady, we thank you for your presence and your blessings.
We thank you for the gift of this new life among us.
We thank you for the joys in our lives, and the many joys to come.
Hail and farewell.

Pathways Ritual

The parents come into the circle from opposite sides, meeting somewhere in the center where a trusted friend waits with the child in his/her arms. The parents take the child & proceed to stand in from of the High Priest and/or Priestess.

High Priestess or Priest:
> Rejoice that our paths have merged this day!
> Rejoice that another's path has just begun!
> Rejoice that many pathways lie ahead.

Parents:
> Our joined paths have brought us much joy,
> But none so great as this.
> Today we ask you to welcome a new traveler -
> A new path seeker sprung from our journey together.

Parents walk around the circle or gathering. As the parents & child pass each member of the gathering, the child should be greeted, good wishes exchanged, etc.

HP/HPS: Welcome traveler!

All: Welcome traveler!

HP/HPS:

> The journey ahead is long, and the path has many branches.
>
> Some paths will flow downhill, some will be a long hard climb.
>
> Although we may have help along the way,
>
> No one can walk our path for us.
>
> This is a hard lesson to be learned as parents.
>
> As you have walked your own path, so too must this new traveler.
>
> The lessons you teach will be a compass.

Parents (to child):

> Fair journey, traveler.
>
> We will guide you with love.

Wish Tree Ritual

This can be used in conjunction with the planting of a new tree to commemorate the child's birth or a "pre-existing" tree can be used. If using a tree that is already planted, as opposed to planting one, simply skip the tree planting portion of the ritual.

This ritual is based on the practice of numerous cultures, including the Native American and Tibetan, which use "Prayer Trees" to focus community energy on a common goal.

Preparations: Have the hole where the tree will be planted dug and ready before the ritual begins. The tree can be chosen according to its meaning, or for characteristics it has that you wish to be bestowed on the child. Each attendee should have written a wish or hope for the new child on a small slip of paper to put on the tree. (See notes at the end of this ritual for suggestions on how to handle this part of the ritual.)

The Ritual:

All attendees gather in a circle around the place where the tree will be planted. The parents & child stand to one side of the hole.

HP: We come together to welcome a newly arrived spirit and to wish her well as she begins her journey. We plant this tree to honor this new child and the Goddess who has sent her to live among us.

The tree is planted, with the parents placing the first handfuls of soil once the tree is in the hole that had been dug for it. Then, others in the circle who wish to do so may add a handful of soil as well. (Or this honor can be reserved for "special" friends and family.) Once the planting of the tree is complete, everyone returns to their original places.

HP: May both child & tree grow strong & true, with deep roots to keep them grounded and branches ever reaching for the sky. Each child who is born carries the hopes and wishes of those who will watch her grow. So it is with this child.

HP (Turns to parents): Upon whom do we set our hopes today?

Parent(s) step forward with the child & tells the name they have chosen for her, along with any other comments they wish to make.

All: Welcome (child's name)

HP: Let us now share our hopes & wishes for (child's name.)

One at a time, the attendees step forward and read their wish/hope out loud. Then, the paper is attached to a branch of the tree.

Once everyone has read their wish/hope & placed it on the tree:

HP: May the hope and joy shared today grow as this tree grows, lasting through countless seasons.

All: So be it.

Suggestions for placing wishes/hopes on tree:

In some cultures, the wishes are left on the tree for a full year. This tradition could be upheld in this case as well by placing each slip of paper in a pre-decorated container (film canisters work well & are readily available. Just go to your local photo lab & ask if they have any. Some people do still use film.) Then, the canisters can be opened and the wishes read again on the child's 1st birthday.

If the papers will only be on the tree for the duration of the ceremony, simply punch a hole in the corner of each paper & string a bit of ribbon through it, then tie it to a branch once the wish has been read.

Afterward, collect the papers & put them in a scrapbook. Besides being a wonderful memento for the parents, this will be something for the child to treasure when she grows older. If planning to save them in this way, you may want to ask each person to put his/her name on their paper.

The Names

A

Abey (F): American Indian; "Leaf."

Abomazine (N): American Indian; "Keeper of the sacred fire."

Acacia (F): Greek; "Thorny, naive."

Acario (M): Latin; "Ungrateful."

Accursius (M): Latin; "To hasten."

Acelin (F): Teutonic; "Noble."

Achall (F): Celtic; In legend, she was a loving sister who died of sorrow when her brother was killed in battle.

Acheflour (F): English; In Arthurian legend, Acheflour was the sister of Arthur & mother of Percival.

Acheron (M): Greek; The river in Hades across which Charon ferries the dead. It is known as the river of woe.

Achikar (M): Assyrian; counselor to the king who was able to accomplish amazing feats using his wisdom.

Achilles (M): Greek; Hero of the *Illiad*. The bravest & strongest of Greek warriors & a hero of the Trojan War. He was invulnerable except at one heel, where his mother held him as she dipped him in the River Styx. He was killed by Paris who shot an arrow in his heel.

Achlys (F): Greek; "Mist; darkness."

Achtland (F): Celtic; A mortal queen who married a giant when she could find no mortal man who met her expectations.

Ackley (M): English; "Meadow of oaks."

Actinia (F): Animal: Sea anemone. From the Greek "aktis" meaning "ray."

Acton (M): English; "Town by the oaks."

Acuzio (M): Latin; "Sharp."

Adair (M): Gaelic; "Exalted; noble."

Adalgisa (F): Germanic; "Noble Hostage."

Adara (F): Greek; "Beauty."

Adonia (F): Greek/Roman; Festival held each year after the harvest to celebrate the death & rebirth of Adonis.

Adonis (M): Greek; A beautiful youth who was a favorite of Aphrodite. As a child, he was put in the care of Persephone, who later refused to give him up. Zeus ruled that Adonis would spend a third of the year with Persephone, a third with Aphrodite & a third on his own. He was later killed by a boar. Zeus granted a request from Aphrodite, allowing Adonis to spend half the year with her & half in the underworld. In this way, he is associated with the natural cycles of life & rebirth.

Adrastea (F): Greek; Nymph who cared for Zeus as an infant.

Adrastos (M): Greek; "Undaunted."

Adriel (N): American Indian; "Beaver." A symbol of skill.

Aed, Aeddon (M): Welsh; "Fire."

Aegir (M): Scandinavian; Sea god. His anger caused storms. He was also the "brew master" for the gods, producing ale for them to drink.

Aegis (M): Greek; The shield of Zeus, later carried by Athena.

Aegle (F): Greek; Name of one of the Hesperides, those who were responsible for guarding the golden apples.

Aeneas (M): Greek; "Worthy of praise." Member of the Trojan Royal family. The Aeneid tells the story of how he escaped after the fall of Troy with his father & of his journey to Italy.

Aeolus (M): Greek; "The changeable one." God of the wind.

Aer, Aeron (F): Welsh; Goddess of war & revenge.

Aesir (M): Scandinavian; One of the two races of Norse Gods, which included Odin, Balder, Loki & Thor, among others.

Aeval (F): Celtic; Goddess of love & sexuality who was later recognized as a fairy queen.

Agatone (M): Greek; "Good; kind one."

Aglaia (F): Greek; "Wisdom; glory." Youngest of the three Graces, she represented splendor.

Agneta (F): Greek; "Pure."

Agora (F): Greek; "Marketplace."

Ahearn (M): Celtic; "Lord of the horses."

Aidan (M): Celtic; Anglicization of Aodhan, meaning "little fire."

Ailill (M): Celtic; Elf.

Aindrea (M): Scottish Gaelic: Form of Andrew, meaning "manly."

Aine (F): Celtic; A moon goddess & fairy queen. It is said she possessed a magical ring that would reveal fairies to the wearer.

Airmid (F): Celtic; a physician in Celtic mythology. It is said that she mourned so deeply for her brother that all the herbs in the world sprung from his grave as she tended it & taught her their uses.

Aislin (F): Celtic/Gaelic; "Dream."

Aither (N): Greek; "Heavenly light."

Aiyana (F): American Indian; "Eternal bloom."

Aiza (N): African (Dahomey); Protective spirit.

Akando (M): American Indian; "Ambush."

Akecheta (M): American Indian; "Warrior."

Alaqua (F): American Indian; "Sweet gum tree."

Alasdair (M): Scottish Gaelic; Form of Andrew, meaning "protector of men."

Alberich (M): Norse; Dwarven king who lived in a beautiful underground palace. He was known for the magical items his people made, including Draupnir, a ring which belonged to Odin.

Alchera (F): Australian Aborigine; Mythical period also

known as "The Dreaming."

Alder (M): Tree; A tree of the birch family. In Norse mythology, the first human couple was made from an ash & an alder. It is often seen as a symbol of regeneration.

Alec, Alexander (M): Greek; "Protector of men."

Alectorian (M): Greek; From the Alectorian stone, a talisman that was said to be found in the belly of a rooster. It was believed to bring health, strength & wealth to the one who carried it.

Alethea (F): Greek; "Truth."

Alexandrite (F): Gemstone; This rare, expensive gem is believed to draw good fortune to the wearer.

Alice (F): English; "Noble; kind." Name of one of the "witches" hanged during the Salem Witch Trials. (Alice Parker)

Allegra (F): Latin; "Cheerful."

Althea (F): Greek; "Healer."

Alvar (M): English; "Elven army."

Alwyn (Var. Aylwin) (M): Welsh; "Friend of the elves."

Amaethon (M): Welsh; God of agriculture.

Amalthea (F): Greek; The mountain goat who nursed Zeus as an infant. One of her horns became the Cornucopia (Horn of Plenty.) She was placed among the stars as the constellation Capricorn.

Amber (F): Gemstone; Actually fossilized tree sap, often containing bits of insects& plants that accidentally got stuck to it. Used for luck, healing, strength, protection against negativity & love.

Amethyst (F): Gemstone; A purple quartz useful for healing, happiness, peace, & to increase psychic awareness. The name is Greek for "not drunken" because they believed it made one immune to the effects of alcohol. Birthstone for the month of February

Amity (F): Latin; "Friendship."

Amnesty (F): English; Pardon of political prisoners. From the Greek "amnesia,'" meaning "forgetting."

Angitia (F): Roman; Early goddess who ruled healing & witchcraft.

Anise (F): Herb; Used to help get rid of nightmares.

Andra (F): Scottish; "Strong & courageous."

Andraste (F): Celtic; A war & nature goddess. Her symbol was the hare.

Andromeda (F): Roman; Daughter of Cassiopeia & Cephus, rescued by Perseus when her father tried to sacrifice her to a sea monster. After her death, she was placed among the stars as a constellation.
Greek; "Leader of men."

Anemone (F): Greek; "Wind flower."

Ann (F): Hebrew; "Gracious." Name of one of the "witches" hanged during the Salem Witch Trials. (Ann Pudeator)

Annawon (N): American Indian; "Chief."

Annora (F): Latin; "Honor."

Annwyl (F): Welsh; "Beloved."

Antigone (F): Greek; Daughter of Oedipus, she defied her uncle, Creon, by performing funeral rites for her brother & was put to death.

Antimony (F): A white metal used to protect from negative energy.

Anu, Anann (F): Celtic; Goddess of plenty, fertility goddess who sometimes formed a trinity with Badb & Macha. Also guardian of cattle & health.

Anubis (M): Egyptian; Jackal-headed god of protection who led the dead to the underworld. Credited with the creation of embalming, which he first performed on Osiris.

Anya (F): Celtic; "Delight."

Aphrodite (F): Greek; Goddess of passionate love.

Apollo (M): Greek/Roman; Twin brother of Artemis, God of the sun. Also associated with music and prophecy. The shrine at Delphi, known for its oracle, was dedicated to him.

Apsu (M): Babylonian; God of fresh water; consort of Tiamat.

Arachne (F): Greek; "spider"; According to legend, she was a young girl who was a skilled weaver. She challenged Athena to a contest. In one version of the story, her weaving was perfect, but depicted some of the gods' less proud moments, such as Zeus abducting Europa. As punishment, Athena turned her to a spider, doomed to weave for eternity.

Aradia (F): Italian; Queen of the witches, daughter of Diana.

Arailt (M): Scottish Gaelic; Form of Harold, meaning "leader of the army.

Arawn (M): Welsh; King of Annwn, the kingdom of the dead.

Ardwina (F): Celtic/Gaelic; A forest goddess. She required that a fine be paid for each animal killed in her forest.

Ares (M): Greek; God of war & one of the twelve major deities of the Greek pantheon.

Argus (M): Greek; "Bright." Giant with one hundred

eyes who was killed by Hermes. His eyes were then placed on the tail feathers of the peacock.

Ariadne (F): Greek; The daughter of King Minos. She helped Theseus to kill the minotaur by giving him a ball of thread. She later eloped with Theseus & was abandoned by him.

Arian (N) Ariana (F): Welsh; "Silver."

Arianrhod (F): Welsh; "Silver Wheel." Beautiful goddess of the stars & reincarnation. Her ship, Oar Wheel, carried dead warriors to Emania.

Arianwen (F): Welsh; "Silver woman."

Aricia (F): Roman; A minor goddess of prophetic visions.

Ariel (N): English; In Shakespeare's "The Tempest," Ariel is a fairy who serves Prospero the magician. Ariel is invisible to all but Prospero & helps him fight the evil seen within the context of the story. Ariel is cheerful, eager to please, & capable of many magical acts.

Arnwald (M): German; "As powerful as an eagle."

Artemis (F): Greek; Goddess of the moon and of wild creatures.

Artorius (M): Latin; "Legendary king."

Asa (F): Japanese; "Born at dawn."

Asgard (M): Scandinavian; In Norse mythology, Asgard is the city of the Gods. It consists of 12 (or more) realms, including Valhalla, the hall of Odin. This region could only be reached from Earth by the rainbow bridge called Bifrost.

Ash (M): Tree; Yggdrasil, the world tree of Norse mythology was an ash, & in Norse myth the first man was formed by the gods from an ash tree. Ash was also used as a cure for warts, or for rickets, & to keep away snakes.

Asteria (F): Greek; The daughter of a Titan. She spurned Zeus' advances & was turned into a quail.

Astarte (F): Phonecian; Fertility goddess often portrayed with cow horns.

Astraea (F): Greek; Goddess of justice & innocence, she became the constellation Virgo.

Athena (Var. Athene) (F): Greek; Warrior goddess & protectress, goddess of wisdom. Her symbols were the olive tree and the owl.

Aubrey (N): English; "Elven king."

Aura (F): Latin; "Wind."
	English; the atmosphere surrounding a person'

Aurora (F): Latin/Roman; "Dawn." Goddess of the dawn & new beginnings.

Avalon (N): Celtic; An island paradise where gods & heroes were fed the apples of immortality. Excalibur was forged on Avalon & it was to Avalon that King Arthur was supposed to have been sent after his death.

Awstin (M): Welsh; "Great; venerable."

Azure (F): English; Sky blue.

B

Badb (F): Celtic; War Goddess & sister of Macha & Anu. Associated with the cauldron, ravens, wisdom.

Baird (M): Celtic/Gaelic; "Minstrel or poet."

Balan (M): Celtic; In Arthurian legend, he met his brother Balin in battle & failing to recognize each other, they killed each other. Merlin buried them in one grave.

Balder (M): Scandinavian; "The Glorious." God of peace and light. Second son of Odin who was killed by his only weakness, mistletoe.

Baldulf (M): English; A knight in some Arthurian legends.

Balin (M): Celtic; In Arthurian legend, he met his brother Balan in battle & failing to recognize each other, they killed each other. Merlin buried them in one grave.

Balius (M): Greek; Horse belonging to Achilles which could speak Greek and often fought at Achilles' side.

Balor (M): Celtic; In mythology, he had a poisonous eye from spying on his father's sorcerers which he had to keep shut at all times. His eye was used as a weapon in battle, when he had it forced open to kill the enemy.

Ban (M): English; In some Arthurian legends, Ban is the father of Lancelot.

Banba (F): Celtic; One of a triad of goddesses that used magic to repel invaders. The other two are Fotia (Fodla) & Eriu.

Banning (M): Gaelic; "Blond child."

Basil (M): Herb; In Celtic, means "Like a King." Regal, kingly.

Bard (M): Celtic; One of a group of minstrels and poets whose tales and songs helped preserve the history, folklore, and myths of many cultures.

Barden (M): English; "Boar's den."

Barklay (M): English; "Birch meadow."

Bast (F): Egyptian; Goddess of protection & cats.

Bastian (M): Greek; "Venerable."

Baxter (M): English; "Baker."

Bedivere (M): Celtic; One of the Knights of the Round table, a loyal companion of King Arthur. It was he who threw Excalibur back into the lake at Arthur's command & took him to the boat that carried him to Avalon.

Bel, Belenus, Belinus (M): Celtic; "Shining." A sun & fire god. From his name we get the name for the celebration Beltane.

Belen (M): Greek; "Arrow."

Belladonna (F): Herb; Once used by witches for astral projection & producing visions. Also used to deaden pain, this herb is reported to have been secretly passed to witches on their way to be burned. Poisonous if taken improperly.
    Italian; "beautiful woman"

Bellanca (F): Greek; "Stronghold."

Bellona (F): Latin; A goddess of war, rites held in her

honor were said the be frenzied & violent.

Beowulf (M): Anglo-Saxon: King of the Geats who vanquished the monster Grendel & his mother for his kinsman Hrothgar. Later in life, he slew a dragon, but died soon after.

Berit (N): German; "Bright; glorious."

Berthold (M): Teutonic; "Glorious ruler."

Bertram (M): English; "Bright raven."

Berwyn (M): Welsh; "Fair headed."

Beryl (F): Gemstone; Used for protection from drowning and seasickness, and for scrying. Birthstone for the month of October.

Bhaltair (M): Scottish Gaelic; Form of Walter, meaning "Ruler of an army."

Biersal (M): German; A kobold who inhabits the cellar & keeps mugs & bottles clean in exchange for a jug of beer each day. If not given his due, he can become a plague on the household.

Birk (M): Celtic; "Birch tree."

Birkita (F): Celtic; "Strength."

Bjorn (M): Scandinavian; "A bear."

Blaine (M): Gaelic; "Thin; lean."

Blair (N): Gaelic; "Child of the fields."

Blathnat (F): Celtic; "Little flower." In some legends, she is the daughter of the high king of the faeries.

Bliss (N): English; "Joy, perfect happiness."

Blodwyn (F): Celtic/Gaelic; "Flower." Created from flowers to be a wife for the god Lleu. She was unfaithful to him & was turned into an owl as a punishment.

Blossom (F): British; "Flower-like."

Bly (N): American Indian; "Tall."

Boann, Boyne (F): Celtic; Goddess of the river of the same name.

Boreas (M): Greek; God of the North wind.

Bowen (M): Celtic/Gaelic; "Archer."

Bragi (M): Scandinavian; Son of Odin, God of poetry. Has the Runes cut into his tongue.

Bran (M): Celtic; From Old Irish *bran* "raven." Bran was the name of a Celtic god in both Irish and Welsh myth. He was a god of prophecy, the arts, & writing.

Brand (M): Scandinavian; "Sword blade."

Branwen (F): Welsh; Goddess of love & beauty.

Breasal (M): Celtic; "Brave, strong in battle."

Brenna (F): Celtic/Gaelic; "Little Raven."

Briar, Brier (F): Plant; a prickly bush.

Brice (M): Celtic; "Quick moving, alert."

Brietta (F): Celtic; "Strong."

Brigantia (F): Celtic; A goddess of rivers, flocks, & fertility.

Brigid, Brigit, Bridgette, Bridget (F): Celtic; "Strength." Warrior goddess & protectress. Also the name of one of the "witches" hanged during the Salem Witch Trials. (Bridget Bishop)

Brina (F): Celtic; "Protector."

Brishen (M): English; "Born during a rain."

Brodie (M): Celtic; From the Irish Gaelic word for "from the ditch."

Brogan (N): Celtic; "Little shoe."

Bronwen (F): Welsh; "Dark & pure."

Brooke (F): German; "A small stream."

Brunhilde, Brynhilde (F): Scandinavian; One of the Valkyries, great female warriors of Norse legend. She defied Odin & was imprisoned.

Bryar (N): English; "From the briar patch."

Bryn (N): Welsh; "Hill."

C

Cabal (M): In some Arthurian legends, Cabal is the name of Arthur's dog.

Cadence (F): Latin; "Melodious."
English: "The beat of any rhythmic action, such as a march, chant, or song."

Cadmus (M): Greek; Ancient king who founded Thebes. Brother of Europa, who was abducted by Zeus. He is often credited with creating the Greek alphabet.

Caelan (M): Gaelic; "Young warrior."

Caer (F): Fairy maiden & goddess of dreams. She appeared as a swan wearing golden necklaces.

Caerleon (F): English; The name of a battle site in Arthurian legend.

Caerwyn (N): Welsh; "White fortress."

Caitlin (F): Celtic/Welsh; "Pure."

Calandra (F): Greek; "Lark."

Calder (M): English; "Stream."

Caley (F): Gaelic; "Slender."

Calista (F): Greek; "Most beautiful."

Callisto (F): Greek; "Most beautiful." Greek moon goddess. In some areas, the she-bear was her sacred animal.

Calixto (M): Latin; "A chalice."

Callidora (F): Greek; "Gift of beauty."

Calliope (F): "One with a beautiful voice." Muse of Epic Poetry. Mother of Orpheus.

Calypso (F): Greek; "One who conceals." A daughter of Atlas, she lived alone on an island, occasionally pulling shipwrecked sailors from the sea.

Camden (M): Scottish; "Winding valley."

Camilla (F): Roman; A virgin queen & worshipper of

Diana. She was known for her speed & grace.

Camlin (M): Celtic; "Crooked line."

Camulos, Camulus (M): Celtic; War god.

Canace (F): Greek; "Child of the wind."

Cara (F): Latin; "Beloved."

Caradoc (F): Welsh; "Friendly."

Cardea (F): Roman; Goddess of the front doorway.

Carden (M): Celtic; "From the black fortress."

Carlin (M): Gaelic; "Little champion."

Carling (N): English; A hill where old women or witches gather.

Carmelide (M): English; Guinevere's father in Arthurian legend.

Carys (N): Welsh; "Love."

Casilda (F): Latin; "Of the home."

Cassair (M): Celtic; "Curly-haired one."

Cassandra, Kassandra (F): Greek; In myth, Cassandra was given the gift of foresight by Apollo, but when she refused his affections, he turned it into a curse, causing others not to believe her warnings.

Cassia (F): Greek; "Champion."

Cayden (M): Gaelic; "Spirit of battle."

Cedric (M): Welsh; "Bounty; spectacle."

Celandia (F): Greek; "A swallow."

Celeste (F): Latin; "Heavenly."

Celestite (F): Gemstone; Used in pyrotechnics.

Cepheus (M): Greek; Husband of Cassiopeia & father of Andromeda, it was he who chained his daughter to a rock as a sacrifice to a sea monster.

Ceres (F): Roman; Goddess of the harvest.

Cernunnos (Kernunnos) (M): Celtic; Horned god & consort of the Lady. His symbols were the stag, the bull, the ram & the horned serpent.

Cerridwen (Keridwen) (F): Welsh; Goddess of the moon & the harvest. She is the keeper of the cauldron of the underworld, in which inspiration and divine knowledge are brewed. Her symbol is a white sow.

Chakra (F): Hindustani; one of the seven energy centers on the human body used in meditation and energy work.

Chandler (M): English; "A maker of candles."

Charis (F): Greek; "Charity." One of the Graces of Greek mythology.

Charissa (F): Greek; "Grace."

Charmian (F): Greek; "Delight."

Chayton (M): American Indian; "Falcon."

Chenoa (F): American Indian; "White dove."

Chilali (N): American Indian; "Snowbird."

Chimalis (N): American Indian; "Bluebird."

Chimera (N): Greek, Mythical beast with the body of a goat, head of a lion & tail of a snake.

Chloe (F): Greek; "Blooming."

Chumani (N): American Indian; "Dewdrop."

Cian (M): Gaelic; "Ancient."

Circe (F): Greek; Daughter of Helios & Perse, a sea-nymph. Circe was a powerful witch who transformed Odysseus' crew into pigs.

Clio (Var. Cleo) (F): Greek; "Glory, fame." Muse of history.

Cliodna (F): Irish; daughter of Manannan's chief druid.

Clota (F): Scottish; Goddess of the river Clyde.

Cocheta (F): American Indian; "That you cannot imagine."

Cocidius (M): Celtic; God of war.

Colleen (F): English; From the Gaelic for "Young girl."

Colm (M): Gaelic; "Dove."

Concordia (F): Latin/Roman; "Harmony; unity." Goddess of concord & harmony.

Conner, Connor (Conan) (M): Celtic/Gaelic; "Wise or knowledgeable."

Consus (M): Latin; God of secret plans & conspiracies.

Coral (F): Gemstone; Word comes from Greek, meaning "daughter of the sea."

Corbett (var. Corbin) (M): Latin; "Raven."

Cordelia (F): Welsh; Daughter of Lyr, the sea god. Often called the May Queen.
        English: From Latin word *cordis*, meaning "Heart."

Coulin (M): Irish; "fairy tunes." Ancient tunes from Ireland which, according to legend, were fairy tunes overheard by bards.

Coventina (F): Celtic; Goddess of springs.

Cresside (F): Greek; "Gold."

Cuchulainn (M): Celtic; son of Lugh, the sun god. His name means "hound of Culann," a title he gained for killing the guard dog of the smith Culann. He was known for his strength & beauty & for having seven fingers on each hand.

D

Dacey (F): Gaelic; "Southerner."

Dagna (F): Germanic; "Beautiful day."

Dagobert (M): Germanic; "Shining sun."

Dahlia (F): Flower;

Daisy (F): Old English; "day's eye." Used in herbal medicine for gout and headaches.

Dakota (N): American Indian; "Friend."

Dallin (M): English; "Pride's people."

Daly (M): Gaelic; "Advisor."

Damara (F): Greek; "Gentle girl."

Damian (M): Greek; "One who tames; fate."

Damona (F): Celtic; An ancient goddess of cattle.

Damona (F): Celtic; An ancient goddess of cattle.

Danae (F): Greek; Mother of the hero Perseus.

Danu, Dannan, Dana (F): Celtic; Possibly the same as Anu. Moon goddess & Mother of the Gods. Patron of fresh water, magic & wisdom.

Darby (M): Gaelic; "Free man."

Darcy (F): Celtic/Gaelic; "Dark one."

Dasan (N): American Indian; "Ruler."

Dawn (F): English; "The time of the rising sun, daybreak."

Delaney (F): Gaelic; "Descendant from the challenger."

Delbin (N): Greek; "Dolphin."

Delight (F): English; "To give great pleasure, to charm."

Delling (M): Scandinavian; "Shining one." God of dawn.

Delphia (F): Greek; Town in which the Oracle of Apollo was located. Also known as Delphi.

Delsin (M): American Indian; "He is so."

Delwyn (F): Welsh; "Pretty & blessed."

Demeter (Var: Demetria) (F): Greek; Earth Mother archetype.

Dermot (M): Celtic; "Envy free."

Desdemona (F): Greek; "Ill-fated one."

Desmond (M): Celtic; "Man of the world."

Destiny (F): Latin; "One's fate."

Devera (F): Roman; Goddess who rules over the brooms used to purify sites before ritual.

Dewitt (M): Welsh; "Blond."

Diana (F): Roman; Moon goddess & Goddess of the hunt. Comparable to Greek Artemis.

Dianthe (F): Greek; "Divine flower."

Dido (F): Greek; Founder of Carthage. Fell in love with Aeneas and, when he left to continue his journey, built a pyre on which she burned herself to death.

Dilys (F): Welsh; "Genuine."

Domhnall (M): Gaelic; "World ruler."

Donagh (F): Celtic; Fairy queen said to be more beautiful than any mortal woman.

Drake (M): English; "A male duck."

Druantia (F): Celtic; "Queen of the Druids." Associated with trees, protection, knowledge & wisdom.

Duff (M): Celtic; "Dark."

Dugan (M): English; "To be worthy."

Dyami (N): American Indian; "Eagle."

Dyani (N): American Indian; "Deer."

Dylan (M): Welsh; A sea god called "Son of the Waves" whose symbol was a silver fish.

Dysis (F): Greek; "Sunset."

E

Eamon (M): Anglo-Saxon; "Wealthy guardian."

Ebon (M): English; "As black as ebony."

Echo (F): Greek; "A repeated voice." Also a nymph in Greek mythology whose longing for Narcissus caused her to waste away till only her voice was left.

Ector, Ektor (M): English; King Arthur's "foster" father in Arthurian legend.

Edan (M): Celtic; "Fire."

Edlyn (F): English; "Noble woman."

Egan (M): Gaelic/Celtic; "Little fire."

Eir (F): Scandinavian; Goddess of healing; considered the greatest of physicians.

Elaine (G): Welsh; Maiden aspect of the triple goddess.

Electra (F): Greek; "The shining one." "Amber"

Elfreda (F): English; "Elf of great strength."

Elgan (M): Welsh; "Bright circle."

Elizabeth (F): Hebrew; "Consecrated to God." Name of one of the "witches" hanged during the Salem Witch Trials. (Elizabeth Howe)

Ellyllon (N): Welsh; A race of beneficial faeries who often enter a household in need, serving as a brownie, helping with household tasks. They remain until offended by a thoughtless act or until their privacy is infringed upon.

Elu (F): American Indian; "Full of grace."

Elva (F): Celtic; Lugh's sister-in-law.

Elvin (M): Anglo-Saxon; "Friend of the elves."

Elysia (F): Latin; "Blissful."

Emania (F): Celtic; Land of the dead, ruled by Macha. "Land of the moon."

Ember (F): English; "The smoldering remains of a fire."

Embla (F): Scandinavian; The name of the first woman, made by the gods from an alder tree.

Emerald (F): Gemstone; A bright green gemstone. In classical mythology, emeralds were believed to be found in the nests of griffins. Birthstone for the month of May.

Emrick (M): Welsh; "Immortal."

Enkidu (M): Babylonian; The archetypal lord of the forests. Preserved in the Epic of Gilgamesh.

Enola (F): American Indian; "Magnolia."

Epona (F): British/Celtic; Goddess of horses.

Erato (F): Greek; Muse of lyric or love poetry.

Erianthe (F): Greek; "Sweet as many flowers."

Erin (Var. Erinn, Eryn, Erynne) (N): Celtic; Name for Ireland.

Eris; "Greek; Goddess of discord.

Eriu (F): Celtic; One of a triad of goddesses that used magic to repel invaders. The other two are Banba & Fodla.

Erlina (F): Celtic; "Girl from Ireland."

Eros (M): Greek; God of romance & passionate love. In some myths, he sprung form an egg laid by Nyx.

Errol (M): Latin; "To wander."

Eryx (M): Greek; A son of Aphrodite & Poseidon.

Esme (F): Latin; "Esteem."

Etain (F): Celtic; Fairy who was turned into a fly & blown around the mortal realm for seven years.

Etania (F): American Indian; "Wealthy."

Eudora (F): Greek; "Good gift." Name of one of the Nereids, one of the sea nymph daughters of Nereus.

Eulalia (F): Greek; "Fair of speech."

Euterpe (F): Greek; Muse of lyric poetry.

Evadne (F): Greek; A water nymph.

Evander (M): Greek; Son of Hermes, helped Aeneas settle Italy.

Ewan (M): Gaelic; "Well born."

Eyota (F): American Indian; "Greatest One."

F

Faina (F): Anglo-Saxon; "Joyful."

Fala (F): American Indian; "Crow."

Farrar (M): Latin; "Blacksmith."

Farrell (M): Celtic; "Courageous."

Fascienne (F): Latin; "Black."

Fauna (F): Roman; Goddess of fertility, farming & chastity.

Fawn (F): English; "A young deer."

Faxon (M): Teutonic; "Long hair."

Fay (F): Latin; "Fairy or elf."

Felicity (F): English; "Good fortune, happiness."

Felicity (F): English; "Good fortune, happiness."

Fennella (F): Gaelic; "White shoulder."

Fenrir (M): Scandinavian; The son of the god Loki, Fenrir is a huge wolf who, according to legend, will swallow Odin at Ragnarok & will be slain by Odin's son, Vidar.

Ferdiad (M): Celtic; Half-brother & friend of Cuchulainn, forced to fight him at one point. The two fought for three days, neither wanting to harm the other, & exchanged food & medicine each night. Eventually, Cuchulainn killed Ferdiad & lamented.

Fergus (M): Celtic; "Of manly strength."

Ffion (M): Welsh; "Foxglove flower."

Fianna (F): Celtic; A group of warriors famed for their courage, strength & courtesy toward women. To be part of the group, men had to agree to a strict code of honor. All the Fianna were also skilled poets.

Fiona (F): Celtic; "White, fair."

Finlay (M): Scottish; "Fair hero."

Flavia (F): Latin; "Blond."

Fletcher (M): English; "Maker of arrows."

Flidais (F): Celtic; goddess of forests & wild creatures. A shape-shifting goddess who rode in a deer-drawn chariot.

Flora (F): Roman; Goddess of spring & birth.

Florian (F): Latin; "Flowering."

Fodla (F): Celtic; One of a triad of goddesses that used magic to repel invaders. The other two are Banba & Eriu.

Forrest (M): English; "Dweller of the forest."

Forseti (M): Scandinavian; "Presiding one." Norse god of justice.

Forsythia (F): English; a shrub with bright yellow blossoms that blooms in spring. Named after botanist William Forsyth.

Fortuna (F): Roman; Goddess of fate.

Freya (F): Scandinavian; Goddess of beauty and love.

Fuchsia (F): English; Plant with bright purple red flowers.

G

Gaia (Var. Gaea, Kaia) (F): Greek; Earth goddess. She & her brother/husband Ouranos were created from the two halves of the shell of Eros' egg. Still used today to refer to the Earth itself, or to the Goddess.

Gage (M): English; "A pledge."

Galahad (M): English; In later versions of Arthurian legend, Galahad is the son of Lancelot & eventually becomes a knight in his own right and who finds the Holy Grail.

Gale (N): Celtic; "Stranger."
    Current usage; "A strong wind."

Galen (M): Gaelic; "Calm."

Galvin (M): Celtic; "Sparrow."

Gannon (M): Celtic: "Of fair complexion."

Garnet (F): Gemstone; This fiery red stone has been

Garnet (F): Gemstone; This fiery red stone has been used throughout history to insure good health. It was also carried by travelers to protect from accidents. Birthstone for the month of January.

Garreth (M): Welsh; uncertain meaning, perhaps means "gentle."

Garridan (M): English; "You hid."

Gavin (M): Welsh; "White hawk."

Gawain (M): Welsh; "Courteous." In Arthurian legend, Gawain was nephew of Arthur.

Gaynor (M): Welsh; "Son of the fair-haired one."

Geirolul (F): Scandinavian; One of the Valkyries, great female warriors of Norse legend.

Geirskogul (F): Scandinavian; One of the Valkyries, great female warriors of Norse legend.

Gelasia (F): Greek; "Predisposed to laughter."

George (M): Greek; "A tiller of the soil." Name shared

by two of the "witches" hanged during the Salem Witch Trials. (George Burroughs & George Jacobs, Sr.)

Gerald (M): Teutonic; "Rules with the spear."

Gerd, Gerda (F): Scandinavian; Giantess associated with beauty & light. Frey became infatuated with her & sent his manservant to (unsuccessfully) woo her.

Gertrude (F): Teutonic; "Spear maiden."

Gethin (M): Welsh; "Dark."

Giles (M): Name of one of the "witches" killed during the Salem Witch Trials. (Giles Corey. He was pressed to death while trying to force a confession.)

Gillian (F): Latin; "Downy-haired."

Glynis (F): Welsh; "Little valley."

Gol (F): Scandinavian; One of the Valkyries, great female warriors of Norse legend.

Goli (F): Scandinavian; One of the Valkyries, great female warriors of Norse legend.

Gondul (F): Scandinavian; One of the Valkyries, great female warriors of Norse legend, it was her job to bring back the spirits of great kings who fell in battle.

Gowan (M): Celtic; from Gaelic *gobha* "a smith".

Grian (G): Celtic; "Sun." A fairy queen with a court on Pallas Green Hill.

Grania (F): Gaelic; "Love."

Grendel (M): In the epic *Beowulf*, Grendel is the monster who repeatedly attacks Hrothgar's hall and is finally killed by Beowulf.

Griffin (M): A creature consisting of the body of a lion, the head and wings of an eagle and (in some legends) the tail of a snake. Considered to be a symbol of power and nobility.

Griffith (M): Welsh; "Fierce chief."

Grigor (M): Welsh; "Watchful."

Gudr (F): Scandinavian; One of the Valkyries, great female warriors of Norse legend.

Guenevere (Gwenhwyfar) (F): Welsh; "white ghost." In Arthurian legend, beautiful but unfaithful wife of Arthur.

Gunnar (Gunther) (M): Norse; Husband of Brunhild (Brynhild), who he won with the help of Siegfried.

Gunnr (F): Scandinavian; One of the Valkyries, great female warriors of Norse legend.

Guth (F): Scandinavian; One of the Valkyries, great female warriors of Norse legend.

Gwydion (M): Welsh; God of enchantment, illusion, magic. A son of Donn, the sea goddess, and brother to Govannon, Arianrhod, and Amaethon (god of agriculture). Known as a great wizard and bard in northern Wales. He was a shape-shifter whose symbol was a white horse.

Gwyneth (F): Celtic; Fortunate, blessed.

Gwynn (M): Welsh; Leader of the Ellyllon. He is traditionally pictured with an owl.

H

Hadden (M): English; "Child of the heather-filled valley."

Hadrian (M): Scandinavian; "Dark one."

Hagan (M): Teutonic; "Strong defense."

Halona (F): American Indian; "Fortunate."

Haltia (N): Finnish; Protective spirits.

Harmony (F): Greek; "A beautiful blending."

Harvey (M): English; "Battle worthy."

Hateya (F): American Indian; "Footprint in the sand."

Hathor (F): Egyptian; Protectress of women in business.

Hecate (F): Greek; Moon goddess associated with the Crone aspect of the Goddess.

Hector (M): Greek; "Anchor; steadfast." In the *Iliad*, Hector is a Trojan prince/hero who is killed by Achilles.

Helaku (N): American Indian; "Sunny day."

Helen (var. Helena, Helene) (F): Greek; Means "torchlight" or "bright one." According to legend, her beauty caused the Trojan War.

Helki (N): American Indian; "To touch."

Hemera (F): Greek; "Daylight."

Henning (M): Teutonic; "Ruler of an estate."

Hera (F): Greek; Goddess of marriage. Wife of Zeus. Her sacred animal was the cow.

Herakles/Heracles (M): Greek/Roman; Son of Zeus. He was known for his strength & bravery, as well as his fighting skill. He became immortal by accomplishing twelve labors.

Hermes (M): Greek; Messenger of the gods. Also seen as god of roads & doorways, & protector of travelers.

Hermione (F): Greek; Daughter of King Menelaus of Sparta & Helen of Troy.

Hervor (F): Scandinavian; One of the Valkyries, great female warriors of Norse legend.

Hestia (F): Greek; Goddess of home & hearth. When both Apollo & Poseidon tried to woo her, she swore to remain a maiden.

Hildr (F): Scandinavian; One of the Valkyries, great female warriors of Norse legend.

Hiorthrimul (F): Scandinavian; One of the Valkyries, great female warriors of Norse legend.

Hlathguth (F): Scandinavian; One of the Valkyries, great female warriors of Norse legend.

Holda (F): Scandinavian; Goddess who cares for children who have died & leads the wild hunt with Odin during Yule. She is considered a patron of witches.

Holden (M): Teutonic; "Gracious."

Holly (F): Plant; Symbolizes hope.

Horus (M): Egyptian; Falcon-headed god of healing & the all-seeing eye. Child of Isis & Osiris; he avenged his father's death. The Pharaohs of Egypt were called the living incarnations of Horus.

Hrist (F): Scandinavian; One of the Valkyries, great female warriors of Norse legend.

Hrothgar (M): In the epic *Beowulf,* Hrothgar is the king of the Danes whose people are being terrorized by the monster Grendel.

Hugin (M): Scandinavian; "Thought." One of Odin's ravens.

Huyana (F): American Indian; "Rain falling."

Hypatia (F): Greek; "Highest."

Hypnos (M): Greek; "Sleep." One of the early Greek gods.

I

Iagan (M): Gaelic; "Little fire."

Ianthe (F): Greek; "Violet colored flower."

Icarius (M): Greek; The first winemaker, taught by Dionysus.

Icarus (M): Greek; Son of Daedalus who escaped Crete with is father by flying with wings his father had made. He flew too close to the sun, causing the wax holding the feathers to melt & plunged to his death into the sea which now bears his name. (Icarian Sea)

Iestyn, Iestin (M): Welsh; Form of Justin, meaning "Lawful; just."

Ignacio (M): Latin; "Lively one."

Ilaria (F): Latin; "Merry one."

Inanna (F): Sumerian; Goddess representation of the mother.

Ingmar (M): Scandinavian; "Famous son."

Ingrid (F): Teutonic; "Hero's daughter."

Iocasta (Var. Jocasta) (F): Greek; Queen who unknowingly wed her son, Oedipus & gave him four children. She committed suicide when she discovered her mistake.

Irene (F): Greek; "Peace." Goddess of peace, daughter of Zeus & Themis.

Iris (F): Plant; A message.
    Greek; Messenger goddess of the rainbow, she served mainly as Hera's errand girl.

Isadora (F): Greek; "Gift of the moon."

Isis (F): Egyptian; Wife & sister of Osiris, associated with love, motherhood, healing, & eternal life. Also associated with the work of magickal spells & charms.

Ismene (F): Greek; Daughter of Oedipus & sister of Antigone, she refused to help her sister perform funeral rites for their brother out of fear of her uncle, Creon.

Isolde (F): Celtic; "Fair one."

Istas (F): American Indian; "Snow."

Ivar (M): Scandinavian; "Warrior; archer."

Ivy (F): Plant; Longevity, fidelity.

J

Jacinda (F): Greek; "Beautiful."

Jacy (F): American Indian; "Moon."

Jade (F): Gemstone; A sacred stone in China, figures of deities were often carved of jade. It is also used as a symbol of love & virtue.

Janus (M): Roman; God of beginnings. Also god of doorways & archways. January is named after him.

Jarvis (M): English; "Servant of the spear."

Jasper (M): Gemstone; This stone comes in various colors, including brown and red. Jasper was used in American Indian rainmaking ceremonies. Birthstone for the month of March.

Jocasta (F): Greek; "Cheerful." Mother & wife of Oedipus.

John (M): Hebrew; "God is gracious." Name shared by two of the "witches" hanged during the Salem by two of the "witches" hanged during the Salem Witch Trials. (John Proctor & John Willard)

Jolon (M): American Indian; "Valley of dead oaks."

Jotnar (M): Norse; Giants who personified the various forces of nature.

Jove (M): An alternate name for Jupiter (Zeus).

Judur (F): Scandinavian; One of the Valkyries, great female warriors of Norse legend.

Juno (F): Roman; Queen of heaven & consort of the god Jupiter.

Jupiter (M): Roman; King of heaven & ruler of the universe.

K

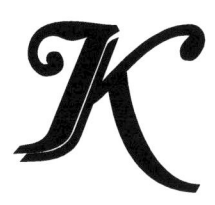

Kachina, Kachine (F): American Indian; "Sacred dancer." Nature spirit found most often among the Pueblo Indians.

Kade (M): Celtic; "Wetlands."

Kaelyn (F): English; "Meadow."

Kaethe (F): Greek; "Pure."

Kai (M): Welsh; A blacksmithing god.

Kaie (F): Celtic; "Combat."

Kalare (F): Latin; "Bright & clear."

Kalika (F):Greek; "Rosebud."

Kaliska (F): American Indian; "Coyote chasing deer."

Kallisto (F): Greek; "Fairest." Sometimes referred to as a nymph. She was a companion of Artemis, who was deceived by Zeus & impregnated by him. Hera turned her into a bear & tricked Artemis into shooting her. Zeus placed her in the sky as a constellation, the bear.

Kara (F): Scandinavian; One of the Valkyries, great female warriors of Norse legend. She was accidentally killed by her husband, Helgi, in battle.

Karma (F): India; The belief that an individual's past actions affect their future lives & experiences. The accumulated good/bad of one lifetime determines one's class, status, character, wealth, etc. in the next incarnation.

Karissa (F): Greek; "Love; grace."

Karsten (M): Greek; "Blessed; anointed one."

Keane (M): English; "Bold."

Kearney (N): Celtic; "Warrior."

Keary (F): Celtic; "Father's dark child."

Keefe (M): Gaelic; "Noble; handsome."

Kei, Kay (M): English; Son of Sir Ector, foster father of King Arthur of Arthurian legend. He becomes one of the knights of the round table.

Keir (M): Celtic; "Dark skinned."

Kelda (F): Scandinavian; "Clear mountain spring."

Kell (M): English; "From the spring."

Kellan (F): Gaelic; "Warrior princess."

Kelsey (N): English; "Victory ship."

Kelvin (M): Gaelic; "From the narrow river."

Kendall (N): Celtic; "Ruler of the valley."

Kendra (F): Anglo-Saxon; "Knowledge."

Kendrick (M): Celtic; "Royal chieftain."

Kenn (M): Welsh; "Clear water."

Kennis (F): Gaelic; "Beautiful."

Kenrich (M): Welsh; "Chief hero."

Kenyon (M): Gaelic; "Blond haired."

Kenzie (N): Scottish; "Light one."

Kern (M): Gaelic; "Dark."

Kerr (M): Scandinavian; "Marshland."

Kiera (F): Gaelic/Celtic; "Small dark one."

Kiernan (M): Celtic; "Son of the master."

Kikimora (F): Russian; Female household spirit who aids busy housewives with their chores, but causes mischief for lazy housewives.

Killian (M): Gaelic; "Fight, strife."

Kincaid (M): Celtic; "Battle chief."

Kiona (F): American Indian; "Brown hills."

Kishi (N): American Indian; "Night."

Kronos (M): Greek; One of the Titans. He & his sister Rhea were the parents of Zeus & Hera. Kronos was warned that he would no longer rule when Hera gave birth to a son by Zeus, so he sought to kill Hera, but his plan was foiled.

Kuan Yin (F): Chinese; Goddess of compassion.

Kyla (F): Gaelic; "Narrow channel."

Kyna (F): Gaelic; "Wise."

Kynthia (N): Greek; "Born under the sign of Cancer."

L

Laertes (M): Greek; King of Ithaca and foster father of Odysseus.

Laila (F): Scandinavian; Night.

Laird (M): Scottish; "Lord."

Lakota (N): Native American; "Friend."

Lamont (M): Scandinavian; "Lawyer."

Lancelot (M): English; In Arthurian legend, Lancelot is one of the greatest of the knights of the round table & a trusted friend of King Arthur. He betrays the king by having an affair with Guinevere, the queen.

Landon (M): English; "Long hill."

Laoghaire (M): Celtic; "Shepherd."

Laraine (F): Latin; "Sea Bird."

Lark (N): Bird; Small bird known for its sweet song.

Latonia (F): Latin; Mother of Diana & Apollo.

Laurel (F): Tree; According to Greek mythology, the nymph Daphne was transformed into a laurel tree while trying to escape Apollo's amorous advances.

Lavender (F): Plant; Known throughout history for its scent & healing & protective properties. Symbolic of longevity, happiness, & peace.

Layna (F): Greek; "Light; truth."

Leander (M): Greek; "Man like a lion." In mythology, Leander swam the Hellespont River every night to visit his love, Hero.

Leandra (F): Greek; "Woman like a lion."

Leda (F): Greek; Lover of Zeus. He seduced her while in the form of a swan.

Leif (M): Scandinavian; "Beloved."

Leith (M): Scottish; "Wide River."

Len (M): American Indian; "Flute."

Lennon (M): Gaelic; "Little cape."

Leonidas (M): Greek; "One who is as bold as a lion."

Letha (F): Greek; "Oblivion."

Letitia (F): Latin; "Joy."

Levana (F): Latin; "Rising sun."

Liadan (F): Celtic; "Grey lady."

Liam (M): Celtic; "Unwavering protector."

Lilac (F): Flower; The lilac has been used in magic to clear bad energy from a space and in medicine to reduce fever.

Lilith (F): Hebrew; Adam's first wife who supposedly became a demoness.

Lily (F): Flower; In many cultures, such as China & India, the lily symbolizes fertility.

Llewellyn (M): Celtic; "Like a lion."

Logan (N): Scottish; "Little hollow."

Loki (M): Scandinavian; Trickster god. After causing the death of Baldur, he was bound by the gods until Ragnarok, when he will be freed.

Lucia (F): Latin; "Light."

Lucifer (M): Italian; Brother of Diana, God of the Sun & Light.

Lucinda (F): Latin; "Bringer of light."

Lucretia (F): Latin; "Bringer of light."

Leulla (F): English; "Elven."

Lugh (M): Celtic; Lughnassadh is named for this god, who was a multi-talented hero. Besides being a great warrior, he was also a gifted carpenter, mason, blacksmith, poet, Druid, etc.

Lulu (F): American Indian; "Rabbit."

Luna (F): Roman; Goddess of the moon.

Lupercus (M): Roman; God of wolves.

Lusmore (M): Irish; "The great herb." In Irish legend, Lusmore was a hunchback whose hump was removed by the fairies.

Lykaios (N): Greek; "Wolf-like."

Lyris (F): Greek; "Player of the lyre."

Lysander (M): Greek; "Liberator."

Lysandra (F): Greek; "Liberator."

M

Maat (F): Egyptian; Goddess of justice & divine order.

Mab (F): Celtic; "Mead." Fairy queen associated with fertility, war & revenge.
: Gaelic; "Joy."

Macaria (F): Greek; Daughter of Hercules & Deianara.

Mace (M): Latin; Aromatic spice derived from the nutmeg plant.

Macha (F): Celtic; Sometimes seen as the Crone aspect of the triple goddess, with Anu & Badb. Associated with ravens & crows. After battles, the Irish would cut off the heads of their enemies & call them "Macha's acorn crop."

Mackenzie (M): Gaelic; "Son of the wise leader."

Macon (M): English; "To make."

Maddock (M): Welsh; "Good fortune."

Madison (N): German; "Son of a great warrior."

Madoc (M): Welsh; Prince said to have discovered America, landing in Alabama in 1170.

Maeve (F): Latin; Goddess.
    Celtic; Queen who brought about the death of Cuchulain by magic & trickery.

Magan (F): Teutonic; "Power."

Magena (F): American Indian; "The coming moon."

Magni (M): Scandinavian; "Strong." One of the sons of Thor.

Magnolia (F): Tree; Tree valued for its fragrant flowers & beautiful leaves.

Magnus (M): Latin; "Large."

Mahala (F): American Indian; "Woman."

Maia (F): Greek; "Nurse; mother."

Mairead (F): Scottish Gaelic; Form of Margaret, meaning "Pearl."

Maisie (F): Scottish; "Child of light."

Maitane (F): English; "Beloved."

Malachite (M): Gemstone; Stone that some legends say will break apart to warn its wearer of coming danger.

Malia (F): American Indian; "Bitter."

Malila (F): American Indian; "Salmon swimming quickly upstream."

Malvina (F): Gaelic; "Smooth snow."

Mansi (N): American Indian; "Plucked flower."

Marduk (M): Babylonian; God of Judgment, hero who destroyed Tiamat.

Maren (F): Latin; "Sea."

Margaret (F): Persian; "Child of light." Name of one of the "witches" hanged during the Salem Witch Trials.

(Margaret Scott)

Margawse (Morgause) (F): Welsh; originally a Mother Goddess, she was transformed in the later Arthurian sagas.

Martha (F): Aramaic; "Lady." Name shared by two of the "witches" hanged during the Salem Witch Trials. (Martha Carrier & Martha Corey)

Mary (F): Hebrew; "Bitter." Name shared by two of the "witches" hanged during the Salem Witch Trials. (Mary Easty & Mary Parker)

Mathilda (F): German; "Battle maiden; strength."

Maura (F): Latin; "Dark."

Meara (F): Gaelic; "Merry."

Meda (F): American Indian; "Priestess."

Medea (F): Greek; "Ruling." In mythology, a famous sorceress who assisted Jason the Argonaut in his quest to get the Golden Fleece. She was the niece of Circe, the great witch & devotee of Hecate.

   Latin; "Middle child."

Meilyr (M): Welsh; "Chief ruler."

Meleager (M): Greek; One of Jason's Argonauts. He was known for his skill as a javelin thrower.

Meli (F): American Indian; "Bitter."

Melia (F): Greek; Nymph who was the daughter of Oceanus.

Melissa (F): Greek; "Honey." A nymph who helped to raise Zeus when he was hidden from his father Cronus.

Mellonia (F): Roman; Goddess of bee keeping.

Melody (F): Greek; "Song."

Melpomene (F): Greek; Muse of tragedy.

Melusina (F): French; Fairy woman who punished her father for slighting her mother by trapping him within a mountain. In turn, she was punished as well, being forced to take the form of a serpent from the waist down every Saturday.

Meredith (F): Welsh; "Protector of the sea."

Merla (F): Celtic; "By the sea." Feminine version of the name Merlin.

Merlin (M): Celtic; "By the sea." Great sorcerer or druid who was said to have learned his magic from the goddess in her various forms. In Arthurian legend, he was Arthur's tutor & mentor.

Merrick (M): English; "Ruler of the sea."

Merrill (M): German; "Famous."

Messina (F): Latin; "Middle child."

Meta (F): Latin; "Ambitious."

Miakoda (F): American Indian; "Power of the moon."

Mica (M): Gemstone; a mineral carried for protection.

Migina (F): American Indian; "Moon returning."

Mimir (M): Scandinavian; God of wisdom & knowledge.

Minda (F): American Indian; "Knowledge."

Minerva (F): Roman; "Power; thinker." Goddess of wisdom, skill, agriculture & war. Comparable to the Greek Athena.

Minka (F): Teutonic; "Strong, resolute."

Minos (M): Greek; King of Crete & son of Zeus & Europa. His wife, Pasiphae was mother of the minotaur.

Mirabelle (F): Latin; "Lovely."

Misae (N): American Indian; "Hot white sun."

Mist (F): Scandinavian; One of the Valkyries, great female warriors of Norse legend.

Mitena (F): American Indian; "New moon."

Mitexi (N): American Indian; "Sacred moon."

Mithra (M): Persian; Sun god & bringer of light.

Modi (M): Scandinavian; "Courage." One of the sons of Thor.

Moira (F): Celtic; "The great."

Mordred, Modred (M): English; In Arthurian legend, he is the son/nephew of King Arthur by the king's half-sister, Morgan la Fey.

Morgan (N) (Var. Morgana, Morganne) (F): Celtic; "Sea Warrior." Goddess of water & magic.

Moriarty (m): Celtic; "Sea warrior."

Morrigan (Morrigu, Morrighan, Morgan) (F) Celtic/Welsh; "Sea-born." A shape-shifting war goddess of lust, magic, prophecy, revenge, war. Known as Great Queen, Supreme War Goddess, Queen of Phantoms, and Specter Queen. Her symbol was the raven.

Motega (M): Native American; "New arrow."

Munin (M): Scandinavian; "Memory." One of Odin's Ravens.

Murphy (M): Gaelic; "Sea Warrior."

Muse (F): The nine sisters who were patrons of the liberal arts & sciences. They are: Calliope, Clio, Erato, Euterpe, Melpomene, Polyhymnia, Terpsichore, Thalia & Urania.

Myrna (F): Gaelic; "Gentle one; polite."

N

Naia (F): Greek; "Flowing."

Naida (F): Greek; "Water nymph."

Nairn (M): Gaelic; ancient name of a river.

Nalren (M): American Indian; "He is thawed out."

Nantan (M): American Indian; "Spokesman."

Narcissa (F): Greek; "Self love." (For more information, see Narcissus.)

Narcissus (M): Greek; "Self love." In mythology, Narcissus turned away the nymph Echo, who pined away until all that was left of her was her voice. As punishment for spurning love, Aphrodite caused him to fall in love with his own reflection in water, where he remained until he died and the Narcissus flower grew where his body lay.

Narella (F): Greek; "Bright one."

Nascha (F): American Indian; "Owl."

Nascha (F): American Indian; "Owl."

Natane (F): American Indian; "Daughter."

Neda (F): Slavic; "Born on Sunday."

Nefertiti (F): Egyptian; "The beautiful one has come."

Neola (F): Greek; "Youthful."

Neoma, Neona (F): Greek; "New moon."

Nerissa (F): Latin; "Daughter of the sea."

Nevin (M): Gaelic; "Worshipper."

Neysa (F): Greek; "Pure."

Niall (M): Celtic; "Champion."

Niamh (F): Celtic; One of Badb's forms, she helps heroes at their death.

Nicneven (F): Scottish; A witch goddess thought to be a

form of Diana. She is said to ride through the countryside with her followers on Samhain.

Nicodemus (M): Greek; "Victory of the people."

Nigel (M): Celtic; "Dark or black."

Nimue (F): Celtic; A moon goddess.

Niobe (F): Greek; "Fern."

Nirvelli (N): American Indian; "Water child."

Nisse/Nissa (F): Scandinavian; "Friendly elf." A helpful household spirit.

Nissyen (M): Celtic "Lover of peace."

Nita (F): American Indian; "Bear."

Nixie (F): German; "Water sprite."

Nodin (N): American Indian; "Wind."

Nokomis (F): American Indian; "Daughter of the moon."

Nolan (M): Gaelic; "Noble."

Nox (F): Roman; Goddess of the night.

Nuit (F): Egyptian; Sky mother.

Nyx (F): Greek; "Night." The first member of the Greek pantheon. It is from Nyx that, according to mythology, the first gods, Eros, Ouranos & Gaia came. forth

O

Oakley (M): English; "From the oak meadow."

Obelia (F): Greek; "Pillar of strength."

Obelix (M): Greek; "Pillar of strength."

Oberon (M): King of the fairies in Shakespeare's "A Midsummer Night's Dream."

Osa (F): Scandinavian; "Small spear."

Odessa (F): Greek; "Journey; voyage."

Odin (Woden, Wodan) (M): Scandinavian; The supreme god of the Norse pantheon. Seen as a protector of heroes & a great magician. According to legend, he only had one eye, having given the other in exchange for wisdom. The wolf & the raven were sacred to him.

Odina (N): American Indian; "Mountain."

Odysseus (M): Greek; "Full of wrath." Hero of the *Od-*

yssey, he was a king of Ithaca & hero of the Trojan War. He wandered for ten years after the fall of Troy before finding his way home.

Ogma (M): Celtic; God who invented Ogham script. Associated with strength, writers, poets, inspiration & creativity.

Okeanos (M): Greek; "Ocean."

Olaf (M): Scandinavian; "Talisman; ancestor."

Olathe (F): American Indian; "Beautiful."

Olrun (F): Scandinavian; One of the Valkyries, great female warriors of Norse legend.

Olympia (F): Greek; "Of Mount Olympus."

Onida (F): American Indian; "Expected one."

Opal (F): Gemstone; In the Middle Ages, Opal was called "eye stone" & was considered beneficial to eyesight. Birthstone for the month of October.

Ophelia (F): Greek; "Useful; wise."

Ophira (F): Greek; "Gold."

Orenda (F): American Indian; "Magical power."

Oriana (F): Latin; "Dawn."

Orinda (F): Teutonic; "Fire serpent."

Orion (M): Greek/Roman; A hunter. Immortalized as a constellation after he was accidentally killed by the goddess Artemis/Diana.

Orla (F): Latin; "Golden woman."

Orpheus (M): Greek; Famous bard, son of Apollo & Calliope. His bride, Eurydice was killed by a snake bite, & Orpheus traveled to the underworld to retrieve her. He managed to charm his way through, using his music to convince Hades to let Eurydice go. However, he ignored Hade's warning not to look back until they had both left the underworld & turned to glance at his bride, only to see her ghost leaving him.

Orrin (M): Greek; "Mountain."

Osiris (M): Egyptian; husband of Isis. Slain by his brother Seth, he was mourned & then returned to life by his wife, Isis. Became god of the underworld.

Oswin (M): English; "Friend of the gods."

Owen (M): Welsh; "Warrior."

P

Pakuna (N): American Indian; "Deer jumping down the hill."

Pan (M): Greek; God of nature, the woods, passion & music. Half man, half goat. Also said in some legends to have invented the flute that bears his name.

Pandora (F): Greek; "Talented one, all gifted." A woman created by the gods to be the wife of Epimetheus, as punishment to mankind for accepting Prometheus' gift of fire.

Panos (M): Greek; "A rock."

Panthea (F): Greek; "Of all the Gods."

Papina (F): American Indian; "Ivy."

Paris (M): Greek; Son of the king of Troy who began the Trojan War by kidnapping Helen, the wife of Menelaus.

Patamon (M): American Indian; "Raging."

Paxton (M): Teutonic; "Trader."

Pearl (F): Gemstone; Symbolic of the moon & of water. Birthstone for the month of June.

Pelagia (F): Greek; "From the sea."

Pembroke (M): Welsh; "From the rocky hill."

Penardun (F): Welsh; Daughter of Don.

Penelope (F): Greek; "Weaver." In mythology, Penelope was the wife of Odysseus, who waited for twenty years for him to return.

Penn (M): English; "Enclosure."

Percival (M): French/English; One of the Knights of the Round table, Percival is the only one to see the Holy Grail.

Perdita (F): Latin; "Lost."

Peregrin (N): English; "Stranger or Traveler."

Persephone (F): Greek; Goddess of the harvest & of the underworld. She was stolen away by Hades to be his wife, & due to the fact that she had eaten a pomegranate seed while in the underworld, she had to remain there for one third of the year. Her story ties into the change of the seasons, as her mother, Demeter, mourns for her while she is in the underworld, thus causing the barrenness of winter.

Perseus (M): Greek; Son of Zeus. He & his mother were set adrift after his birth in an attempt to foil a prophecy that said he would kill his grandfather, King Acrisius. He saved Andromeda from being sacrificed to a sea serpent by turning it to stone with the head of a Gorgon.

Phedra (F): Greek; "Shining one." Daughter of Minos, third wife of Theseus.

Phelan (M): Gaelic; "Little wolf."

Philana (F): Greek; "Adoring."

Philippa (F): Greek; "Lover of horses."

Philomena (F): Greek; "Lover of the moon."

Phoebe (F): Greek; "Bright one."

Phoenix (N): Greek; Mythological bird reborn from its own ashes. A symbol of reincarnation.

Pilan (N): American Indian; "Supreme essence."

Pixie (F): Celtic; "Small fairy."

Poloma (F): American Indian; "Bow."

Polyhymnia (F): Greek; Muse of sacred poetry or mime.

Poseidon (M): Greek; God of the sea.

Prometheus (M): Greek, "Forethinker." He brought fire to mankind, in defiance of Zeus. As punishment, he was chained to a mountain where an eagle would come each day to eat his entrails, only to have them restored each night. His shackles were finally broken by Herakles.

Proteus (M): Greek; "The old man of the sea." A shape-shifting sea god & prophet, he disliked sharing information with mortals & had to be captured before he would answer any questions.

Pryderi (M): Welsh; "Concern; caring for."

Psyche (F): Greek; "The soul."

Pythia (F): Greek; "Prophet." A serpent goddess & child of Gaia.

Q

Quella (F): English; "Pacify."

Quenby (F): Scandinavian; "Womanly."

Quest (M): English; A journey with a specific goal, marked with trials that must be overcome. .

Quillan (M): Gaelic; "Cub."

Quillon (M): Latin; "Sword hilt."

Quinlan (M): Celtic; "Well shaped; athletic."

Quinn (M): Celtic; "Wise."

R

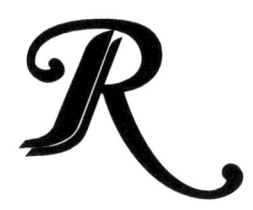

Ra (M): Egyptian; Sun god.

Radella (F): English; "Elven advisor."

Ragnar (M): Scandinavian; "Wise leader."

Ragnhild (F): Scandinavian; "One who is wise in battle."

Rainier (M): Latin; "Ruler."

Ramla (F): Egyptian; "Seer of the future."

Randolph (M): Scandinavian; "Shield wolf."

Rane (F): Scandinavian; "Queen; pure."

Rathgrith (F): Scandinavian; One of the Valkyries, great female warriors of Norse legend.

Raven (N): Bird; In Native American lore, Raven is a trickster and, often, hero.

Raynor (M): Scandinavian; "Mighty army."

Rebecca (F): Hebrew; "Tied." Name of one of the "witches" hanged during the Salem Witch Trials. (Rebecca Nurse)

Redrick (M): Germanic; "Counsel power."

Reece (M): Welsh; "Enthusiastic."

Reese (N): Welsh; "Ardent."

Regan (N): Celtic; "Royal."
       Gaelic; "Little king."

Reginlief (F): Scandinavian; One of the Valkyries, great female warriors of Norse legend.

Remus (M): Latin; "Swift oarsman." One of the brothers credited with the founding of Rome.

Renata (F): Latin; "Reborn."

Rhea (F): Greek; One of the Titans, wife of Cronus & mother of Hera & Zeus, among others.

Rhiamon (F): Welsh; "Witch."

Rhiannon (F): Roman; Goddess of the underworld, also symbolic of fertility.
          Welsh; "Great queen." Goddess of birds & horses.

Rhoswen (F): Gaelic; "White Rose."

Rhys (N): Welsh; "Ardor."

Riordan (M): Gaelic; "Poet."

Risa (F): Latin; "Laughter."

Roane (N): Scottish; Gentle fairy race who look like seals.

Roarke (M): Gaelic; "Famous ruler."

Rogan (N): Gaelic; "Red haired."

Romulus (M): Latin; One of the brothers credited with the founding of Rome.

Ronan (M): Celtic; "A pledge."

Rory (N): Gaelic; Red king."

Rosemary (F): Plant; Symbolizes remembrance. Used medicinally for headaches, tension & insomnia.

Rota (F): Scandinavian; One of the Valkyries, great female warriors of Norse legend.

Rowan (N): Plant; One of the trees sacred to the Druids, thought to protect against enchantment & evil spirits.

Rowena (F): Celtic; "Slender & fair."

Ruby (F): Gemstone; Symbolic of fiery passion. Birthstone for the month of July.

Rue (F): Herb; Associated with grief and remorse, this herb is also used to treat mild pain and for protection against enchantment.

S

Sabola (F): Egyptian; "Prophetess."

Sabrina (F): Latin; "From the borderland."

Sage (M): Latin; "Prophet." Also an herb burned for cleansing.

Sahale (N): American Indian; "Above."

Sakari (N): American Indian; "Sweet."

Salina (F): Latin; "By the salt water."

Samuel (M): Hebrew; "Asked of God." Name of one of the "witches" hanged during the Salem Witch Trials. (Samuel Wardwell)

Sandrine (F): Greek; "Helper & defender of mankind."

Sangridr (F): Scandinavian; One of the Valkyries, great female warriors of Norse legend.

Sapphire (F): Gemstone; Its deep blue makes it a good stone for meditation & relaxation. Used to being health and wealth. Birthstone for the month of September.

Sarah (F): Hebrew; "Princess." Name shared by two of the "witches" hanged during the Salem Witch Trials. (Sarah Good & Sarah Wildes)

Saraide (F): Celtic; "Excellent."

Satinka (F): American Indian; "Magic dancer."

Saxon (M): English; "Swordsman."

Sayer (M): Welsh; "Carpenter."

Scully (M): Celtic/Gaelic; "Town crier."

Sebastian (M): Greek; "Majestic."

Selene (Var. Selena, Selinda) (F): Greek; Goddess of the moon.

Selina (F): Greek; "Lunar glow."

Semele (F): Latin; "Once." Mother of Dionysus.

Serenity (F): The state of being calm, peaceful, or tranquil.

Shako (N): American Indian; "Mint."

Shannon (N): Irish; "Wise one."

Shayla (F): Celtic; "Fairy palace."

Shea (M): Irish; "Hawk-like; stately."

Sheehan (M): Gaelic; "Little peaceful one."

Shela (F): Celtic; "Musical."

Sheldon (M): English; "Protected hill."

Sheridon (M): Celtic; "Wild one."

Sibyl (var. Sibylle, Cybil) (F): Greek; "Prophetess."

Sidra (F): Latin; "Like a star."

Sigrdrifa (F): Scandinavian; One of the Valkyries, great female warriors of Norse legend.

Sigrlinn (F): Scandinavian; One of the Valkyries, great female warriors of Norse legend.

Sigrun (F): Scandinavian; One of the Valkyries, great female warriors of Norse legend.

Silva (F): Latin; "Woodland maid."

Silvanus (M): Roman; "He of the forest." God associated with forest & parklands.

Sinead (F): Celtic; "Gracious."

Skuld (F): Scandinavian; One of the three Norns, the goddesses who weave the Web of the Wyrd. Skuld is the youngest & represents the future.

Slade (M): English; "Child of the valley."

Slevin (M): Gaelic; "Mountaineer."

Sloan (M): Gaelic; "Warrior."

Sofi, Sophie (F): Greek; "Wisdom."

Solace (F): Latin; "Comfort."

Solita (F): Latin; "Alone."

Solitude (F): The state of being alone or in seclusion.

Sophie (F): Greek; "Wisdom."

Sophronia (F): Greek; "Foresighted."

Sora (F): American Indian; "Singing bird soars."

Sorcha (F): Gaelic; "Bright."

Storme (M): Derivative of Storm; a weather disturbance marked by rain, winds, thunder & lightning.

Susannah (F): Hebrew; "Lily." Name of one of the "witches" hanged during the Salem Witch Trials. (Susannah Martin)

Svafa (F): Scandinavian; One of the Valkyries, great female warriors of Norse legend.

Svipul (F): Scandinavian; One of the Valkyries, great female warriors of Norse legend.

Sweeny, Sweeney (M): Gaelic; "Little hero."

T

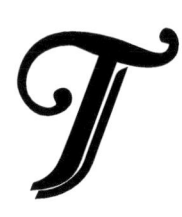

Tabitha (F): Greek; "Gazelle."

Taborri (F): Native American; "Voices that carry."

Tacincala (F): Native American; "Deer."

Tacita (F): Latin; "To be silent."

Tadi (N): American Indian; "Wind."

Taima (F): American Indian; "Crash of the thunder."

Tainn (N): American Indian; "New moon."

Taipa (N): American Indian; "To spread wings."

Takoda (N): American Indian; "Friend to all."

Tala (F): American Indian; "Wolf."

Talasi (F): American Indian; "Corn-tassel flower."

Talasi (F): American Indian; "Corn-tassel flower."

Talfryn (N): Welsh; "From the high end of the hill."

Talia (F): Greek; "Blooming."

Taliesin (M): Welsh; Means "radiant brow." God of magic, music, wisdom, writing. Known as Prince of Song, Chief of the Bards of the West, and Patron of Druids, he was a great magician, bard, and shape-shifter who gained his knowledge from the goddess Cerridwen. herself.

Tallulah (F): American Indian; "Leaping Water."

Talos/Talus (M): Greek; Giant who protected Crete.

Tama (F): American Indian; "Thunderbolt."

Tangwystl (F): Welsh; "Pledge of peace."

Tania (F): Latin, A Fairy Queen.

Tansy (F): Greek; "Immortality."

Tara (F): Celtic; "Tower."

Tartaros (M): Greek, "Underworld."

Tate (M): English; "To be cheerful."

Taurin (N): Latin; "Born under the sign of Taurus."

Tavis, Tevis (M): Scottish; "Twin."

Tawana (N): American Indian; "Created."

Tawny (F): English; "Tan or light brown in color."

Tayen (N): American Indian; "New moon."

Teagan (N): Celtic; "Attractive."

Teague (M): Celtic/Gaelic; "Poet."

Tegau (F): Welsh; "Pretty."

Tegwyn (F): Welsh; "Lovely maiden."

Tehya (F): American Indian; "Precious."

Terena (F): Latin; "Earthly."

Terentia (F): Greek; "Guardian."

Terminus (M): Roman; God of sacred space & the boundaries thereof.

Terpsichore (F): Greek; Muse of Dancing & choral song.

Terra (F): Latin; "Earth."

Terrel (M): English; Thunderer."

Tess (F): Greek; "To reap."

Tethys (F): Greek; "Nurse." Wife of Oceanus.

Thadea (F): Greek; "Brave, courageous."

Thalassa (F): Greek; "From the sea."

Thalia (F): Greek; "Blooming; plentiful." Muse of comedy.

Thane (M): English; "Attendant warrior."

Thanos (M): Greek; "Noble."

Thea (F): Greek; An early goddess of light.

Theodoric (M): Teutonic; "Ruler of the people."

Theone (N): Greek; "Godly."

Thera (F): Greek; "Wild."

Theron (M): Greek; "Hunter."

Thierry (M): Teutonic; "People's ruler."

Thisbe (F): Greek; "Where the doves live."

Thor (M): Scandinavian; God of the sky & thunder.

Thora (F): Scandinavian; "Thunder."

Thorne (M): English; "Thorn tree."

Thoth (M): Egyptian; God of reincarnation & writing.

Thrud (F): Scandinavian; One of the Valkyries, great female warriors of Norse legend.

Thurston (M): Scandinavian; "Thor's stone."

Thyra (F): Greek; "Shield-bearer."

Tia (F): Greek; "Princess."

Tiamat (F): Babylonian; Dragon Goddess of salt waters & mother of all other Gods & Goddesses of Babylon (excepting Apsu, her consort.) She was eventually destroyed by Marduk & her body became the basis for the universe as we know it.

Tibalt (M): Greek; "People's prince."

Tiernan (Tierney) (N): Celtic; "Lordly."

Timeus (M): Greek; "Perfect."

Timon (M): Greek; "Worthy."

Titania (F): Greek; "Giant." In Shakespeare's "A Midsummer Night's Dream," Titania is the queen of the fairies.

Titus (M): Greek; "Of the giants."

Todd (M): English; "Fox."

Tora (F): Scandinavian; "Thunder."

Torin (M): Celtic; "Chief."

Treasa (F): Celtic; "Strong."

Trent (M): Latin; "Torrent."

Treva (F): Celtic; "Prudent."

Trista (F): Latin; "Sorrowful."

Tristan (Var. Drystan) (M): Welsh; "Sad."

Tryphena (F): Latin; "Dainty."

Typhon (M): Greek; Child of Gaia & Tartaros. Typhon was a creature with a hundred serpent heads & a terrifying voice whose eyes poured forth fire. He tried to overthrow Zeus.

Tyr (M): Scandinavian; God of war & justice. Younger brother of Thor.

U

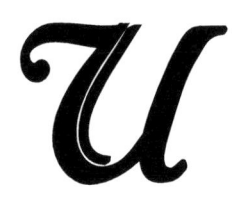

Ula (F): Celtic; "Sea Jewel."

Uland (M): Teutonic; "Noble country."

Uldra (F): Scandinavian; Shy and generally benevolent fairy race.

Ulf (M): Teutonic; "Wolf."

Ulrich (M) English/German; "Wolf ruler."

Ulrika (F): English/German; "Wolf ruler."

Ultima (F): Latin; "Aloof."

Ulysses (M): Latin; "Wrathful."

Una (F): Latin; "One."

Undine (F): A water spirit who could choose to gain a soul by marrying a mortal man and bearing his child.

Unity (F): English; "Togetherness, harmony between people."

Urania (F): Greek; "Heavenly." Muse of astronomy.

Urd (F): Scandinavian; One of the three Norns, the goddesses who weave the Web of the Wyrd. Urd is the eldest & represents the past.

Urien (M): Celtic; "Privileged birth."

Ursula, Ursala, Ursa (F): Latin; "Female Bear."

Uther (M): English; In Arthurian legend, Uther is the father of King Arthur.

V

Val (N): Latin; "Power."

Vala (F): English; "Chosen."

Valda (F): Scandinavian; "Spirited warrior."

Valencia (F): Latin; "Bravery."

Valtin (M): Latin; "Good health."

Valerian (M): Plant; Symbolizes readiness. Used medicinally as a sedative.

Valiant (M): Bold, brave, courageous.

Valkyrie (F): Norse; Female attendants of Odin, often female warriors, who take the souls heroes killed in battle to Valhalla where the Valkyries then served them at the table.

Valonia (F): Latin; "Of the vale."

Valora (F): Latin; "The valorous."

Vance (M): English; "Marshes."

Vanir (M): Scandinavian; One of the two races of gods in Norse mythology. The Vanir included Frey & Njord.

Vasilios (M): Greek; "Of royal blood."

Vaughn, Vaughan (M): Celtic; "Small."

Venus (F): Roman; Goddess of love & romance.

Vera (F): Latin; "True."

Verdandi (F): Scandinavian; One of the three Norns, the goddesses who weave the Web of the Wyrd. Verdandi is the middle goddess & represents the present.

Verity (F): Latin; "Truth."

Vernon (M): Latin; "Youthful."

Vervain (N): Plant; Vervain is known for its healing

properties, especially for women's problems. It was sacred to Venus.

Vesper (F): Latin; "Evening."

Vesta (F): Roman; Goddess of fire.

Vevila (F): Gaelic; "Woman with a melodious voice."

Violet (F): Plant; Loyalty, devotion, and faithfulness.

Virgil (M): Latin; "Strong."

Viveca (F): Germanic/Swedish; "War."

Voleta (F): Greek; "Veiled one."

W

Walden (M): Teutonic; "Mighty."

Wakanda (N): American Indian; "Inner Magical power."

Waneta (F): American Indian; "Charger."

Wapeka (N): American Indian; "Skillful."

Warren (M): English; "Keeper of a game preserve."

Wendy (F): Teutonic; "Fair one."

Whitby (M): Scandinavian; "Farm with white walls."

Willa (F): Teutonic; "Fierce protector."

Willow (F): Plant; Symbolizes sadness. The bark of this tree is known for reducing inflammation in the joints & for reducing fever.

Wilmott (M): Name of one of the "witches" hanged during the Salem Witch Trials. (Wilmott Redd)

during the Salem Witch Trials. (Wilmott Redd)

Wilona (F): English; "Desired."

Winema (F): American Indian; "Female Chief."

Winona (F): American Indian; "First-born daughter."

Wolfgang (M): Teutonic; "Wolf strife."

Wolfram (M): Teutonic; "Wolf raven."

Wyn, Wynn, Wynne (M): Welsh; "White; fair."

Wyome (N): American Indian; "Plain."

X

Xanthe, Xanthus (M): Greek; "Yellow."

Xavier (M): Latin; "Savior."

Xena (F): Greek; "Welcome guest."

Xenia (F): Greek; "Hospitality."

Xenos (M): Greek; "Stranger."

Xylia (F): Greek; "Wood dweller."

Xylia, Xylona (F): Greek; "From the forest."

Y

Yahto (M): American Indian; "Blue."

Yakecan (N): American Indian; "Sky."

Yancy (M): American Indian; "Englishman."

Yepa (F): American Indian; "Winter princess."

Yolanda (F): Latin; "Violet flower."

Yorath (M): Welsh; "Handsome lord."

York (M): Celtic; "From the farm of yew trees."

Yuma (M): American Indian; "Son of the chief."

Z

Zahur (M): Egyptian; "A flower."

Zaltana (F): American Indian; "High mountain."

Zandra (F): Greek; "Helper & defender of mankind."

Zea (F): Latin; "Wheat."

Zelda (F): Teutonic: "Female warrior."

Zelia (F): Greek; Zeal.

Zelinda (F): German; "Shield of victory."

Zena (F): Greek; "Alive."

Zenaide, Zenobia (F): Greek; "Given life by Zeus; Daughter of Zeus."

Zeth (M): Greek; "Investigator."

Zeus (M): Greek; Ruler of the Greek pantheon, a title he gained by overthrowing his father, Kronos.

Zeva (F): Greek; "Sword."

Zoe (F): Greek; "Life."

Zoilo (M): Greek; "Lively."

Index of Names by Meaning (Stated or Implied)

Index of Names by Meaning
(Stated or Implied)

Abundance/Fertility: Amalthea, Anu, Anann, Astarte, Brigantia, Cedric, Ceres, Cerridwen, Demeter, Demetria, Flora, Freyr, Fauna, Inana, Lily, Mab, Mabon, Persephone, Rhiannon, Tess, Thalia

Adoration: Philana

Advisor: Daly, Radella, Redrick

Alone: Solita, Solitude, Una

Ambition: Meta

Ambush: Akando

Ancestor: Olaf

Archery/Arrow: Belen, Bowen, Fletcher, Ivar, Motega, Polama

Army: Alvar, Arailt, Bhaltair

Arts (Dance/Music/Song/Poetry): Baird, Bard, Bragi, Bran, Cadence, Calliope, Erato, Euterpe, Fianna, Harmony, Kachona, Kachine, Len, Lugh, Lyris, Melody, Melpomene, Muse, Ogma, Orpheus, Pan, Polyhymnia, Riordan, Satinka, Shela, Taliesin, Teague, Terpsichore, Thalia

Bear: Bjorn, Nita, Quillan, Ursula, Ursala, Ursa

Beast: Chayton, Chenoa, Chilali, Chimalis, Colm, Corbett, Delbin, Dyami, Dyani, Lupercus, Lykaios, Quillan, Tod

Beauty: Adara, Adonis, Aphrodite, Arianrhod, Balder, Belladonna, Branwen, Calista, Calisto, Callidora, Calliope, Camilla, Charissa, Dagna, Delwyn, Donagh, Ellyllon, Eulalia, Fiona, Gerd, Gerda, Guinivere, Harmony, Isolde, Jacinda, Kallisto, Kennis, Mirabelle, Nefertiti, Olathe, Rowena, Teagan, Tegau, Tagwyn, Yorath

Beaver: Adriel

Beginning: Janus

Beloved: Annwyl, Cara, Maitane

Birch: Barklay, Birk

Bird: Asteria, Bertram, Bran, Brenna, Caer, Calandra, Celandia, Chayton, Chenoa, Chilali, Chimalis, Colm, Corbett, Drake, Dyami, Fala, Galvin, Gavin, Horus, Laraine, Lark, Leda, Macha, Nascha, Raven, Shea, Sora, Thisbe

Bitter: Malia, Mary, Meli

Blond: Banning, Berwyn, Dewitt, Kenyon

Blue: Azure, Yahto

Bluebird: Chimalis

Boar: Barden

Boundaries: Cardea, Penn, Terminus

Brave: Achilles, Breasal, Dalaney, Herakles, Keane, Leandra, Leonidas, Perseus, Thadea, Valencia, Valora

Bright: Argus, Berit, Bertram, Elgan, Helen, Helena, Helene, Kalare, Narella, Phoebe, Sorcha

Celebration: Adonia

Champion: Carlin, Cassia, Ingrid, Niall, Nicodemus, Sweeny, Sweeney

Chief: Annawon, Griffith, Kendrick, Kenrich, Kincaid, Torin, Winema

Chosen: Vala

Comfort: Solace

Courage: Andra, Breasel, Brunhilde, Farrell, Keane, Kearney, Leander, Leandra, Leonidas, Llewellyn, Modi, Niall, Thadea

Courteous: Gawain, Holden, Myrna, Sinead

Creativity: Baird, Calliope, Cerridwen, Clio, Muse, Ogma, Pan, Pandora, Taliesin, Tawana, Thalia

Crow: Fala

Dainty: Tryphena, Vaughn, Vaughan

Darkness: Achlys, Bronwen, Carden, Consus, Darcy, Duff, Ebon, Fascienne, Gethin, Hadrian, Keary, Keir, Kern, Kiera, Kishi, Laila, Liadan, Maura, Nigel, Nox, Nyx, Osiris

Daughter: Blathnat, Coral, Cordelia, Hermione, Ingrid, Ismene, Makaria, Melia, Netane, Nokomis, Penardun, Winona, Zenaide, Zenobia

Dawn: Asa, Aurora, Delling, Oriana

Deer: Dyani, Fawn, Kaliska, Pakuna, Tacincala

Defiance: Antigone, Ariadne, Asteria, Brunhilde, Brynhilde, Icarus, Prometheus

Desire: Wilona

Directional: Dacey, Sahale

Dog: Cabal

Dolphin: Delbin

Dove: Chenoa, Colm, Thisbe

Dream: Aislin, Alchera, Caer

Duck: Drake

Eagle: Arnwald, Dyami

Expected: Onida

Evening: Vesper

Fair: Fiona, Finlay, Gannon, Gaynor, Isolde, Kallisto, Kenzie, Wendy, Wyn, Wynn, Wynne

Falcon: Chayton

Fame: Ingmar, Merrill, Roarke

Father: Ban. Cephus, Ector, Ektor, Odin, Uther

Fern: Niobe

Fertility/Abundance: Amalthea, Anu, Anann, Astarte, Brigantia, Cedric, Ceres, Cerridwen, Demeter, Demetria, Flora, Freyr, Fauna, Inana, Iris, Kalika, Lily, Mab, Mabon, Persephone, Rhiannon, Rhoswen, Susannah, Tess, Thalia

Flower: Anemone, Aiyana, Blathnat, Blodwyn, Blossom, Chloe, Dahlia, Dianthe, Erianthe, Ffion, Florian, Flora, Fuchsia, Hadden, Ianthe, Lily, Mansi,

Talasi, Talia, Violet, Yolanda, Zahur

Fly: Etain, Taipa

Forest: Ardwina, Enkidu, Flidais, Forrest, Herne, Holda, Silva, Silvan, Xylia, Xylona

Freedom: Amnesty, Darby, Lysander, Lysandra

Friendship: Alwyn, Amity, Caradoc, Dakota, Elvin, Lakota, Nissa, Oswin, Takoda

Fortune/Fate/Luck: Alexandrite, Amber, Aricia, Atropos, Damian, Desdemona, Destiny, Felicity, Fortuna, Gwyneth, Halona, Karsten, Klotho, Lachesis, Maddock, Skuld, Urd, Verdandi

Fox: Todd

Gazelle: Tabitha

Giant: Gerd, Gerda, Talus, Titania, Titus

Gold: Cresside, Ophira, Orla

Grace: Camilla, Charissa, Elu, Karissa

Great: Awstin, Bastian, Eyota, Moira, Saraide, Sebastian, Walden

Happiness: Allegra, Amethyst, Anya, Bliss, Charmian, Concordia, Delight, Elysia, Faina, Felicity, Gelasia, Ignacio, Ilaria, Lavender, Letitia, Mab, Meara, Reece, Risa, Tate

Hawk: Gavin, Shea

Healing/Health: Airmid, Alectorian, Althea, Amber, Amethyst, Angitia, Anu, Anann, Eir, Garnet, Horus, Isis, Tethys, Valtin, Vervain

Herbs: Anise, Belladonna, Shako, Valerian, Vervain

Hill: Bryn, Carling, Kiona, Landon, Talfryn

Honor(able): Annora, Awstin, Bastian, Esme, Fianna, Honora

Hope: Holly

Horse: Ahearn, Balius. Epona, Gwydion, Philippa, Rhiannon

Hospitality: Xena, Xenia

Hunter: Artemis, Diana, Herne, Holda, Orion, Theron

Immortal: Emrick, Tansy

Innocence: Astraea,

Intelligence: Consus, Druantia, Grigor

Ivy: Papina

Justice: Astraea, Dharma, Forseti, Iestin, Iestyn, Karma, Lamont, Maat, Themis, Tyr

Kindness: Agatone, Alice, Charis, Damara, Kuan Yin, Myrna, Pryderi

Lady: Martha

Large: Magnus

Lark: Calandra

Leadership: Andromeda, Annawon, Arailt, Arthur, Berthold, Bhaltair, Kinkaid, Marduk, Ragnar

Leaf: Abey

Light: Aither, Argus, Aurora, Bel, Belenus, Belinus, Berit, Dagobert, Dawn, Delling, Electra, Fennella, Gerd, Gerda, Grian, Helaku, Helen, Helene, Helena, Hemera, Layna, Levana, Lucia, Lucifer, Lucinda, Lucretia, Maisie, Misae, Margaret, Narella, Phaedra

Lily: Susannah

Lost: Perdita

Love: Aeval, Amber, Annwyl, Aphrodite, Branwen, Cara, Carys, Erato, Eros, Freya, Freyja, Grania, Isis, Jade, Kalare, Karissa, Kenyon, Kenzie, Leander, Leif, Narcissa, Narcissus, Pan, Rhys, Ruby, Venus

Loyalty: Bedivere, Dakota, Fauna, Ferdiad, Hector, Isis, Ivy, Violet

Magnolia: Enola

Manly: Aindrea, Fergus

Memory: Munin, Rosemary

Messenger: Hermes, Iris, Nantan, Scully

Mother: Acheflar, Adrastea, Amalthea, Danae, Demeter, Igraine, Isis, Latonia, Maeve, Maia, Margawse, Morgause, Nuit, Rhea, Tiamat

Mountain: Orrim, Slevin, Zaltana

Mystic: Aradia, Aricia, Banba, Circe, Cocheta, Damian, Danu, Darcy, Delsin, Destiny, Echo, Elaine, Eriu, Fodla, Gwydion, Hecate, Hekate, Holda, Isis, Nicneven, Orenda, Rhiamon, Satinka, Taliesin, Wakanda

Noble/Nobility: Acelin, Achtland, Adair, Adalgisa, Aeneas, Ahearn, Alice, Aradia, Artorius, Basil, Bedivere, Berthold, Cadmus, Dasan, Desmond, Diana, Druantia, Ector, Edlyn, Ewen, Eyota, Griffin, Hypatia, Keefe, Kellan, Kendall, Kendrick, Laird, Nolen, Thanos, Tiernan, Uland, Urien

Oak: Ackley, Acton, Oakley

Oblivion: Letha

Owl: Nescha

Passion: Aphrodite, Eros, Ruby, Venus

Peace: Amethyst, Colm, Concordia, Freyr, Galen, Irene, Lavender, Nissyen, Quella, Sapphire, Serenity, Sheehan, Tangwystl, Valerian

Pearl: Mairead

Perfect: Timeus

Perseverence: Adrastos, Cian, Clio, Hector, Malila, Reese

Pledge: Gage, Ronan, Tangwystl

Power: Magan, Redrick, Val

Precious: Tehya

Prophecy: Apollo, Aricia, Bran, Cassandra, Delphia, Kassandra, Pythia, Ramla, Sabola, Sage, Sibyl, Sophronia

Protection: Adrastea, Aegis, Aegle, Alasdair, Alec,

Alexander, Amber, Antimony, Anubis, Athena, Aiza, Bast, Bastet, Bellanca, Beryl, Brigid, Brina, Dagda, Druantia, Eamon, Garnet, Grigor, Hagan, Haltia, Hathor, Holda, Liam, Meredith, Mica, Rowan, Rue, Sandrine, Sheldon, Talos, Terentia, Thyra, Willa, Zander

Purity: Agneta, Bronwen, Caitlin, Devera, Elaine, Fauna, Hestia, Kaethe, Neysa, Percival, Rane

Raven: Bertram, Bran, Brenna, Corbett, Macha, Wolfram

Rebirth/Regenration: Adonia, Alder, Flora, Isis, Osiris, Phoenix, Renata, Thoth

Red: Rogan, Rory

Ruler: Achtland, Alberich, Arawn, Arthus, Artorius, Aubrey, Berthold, Bhaltair, Cadmus, Dasan, Domhnall, Druantia, Gerald, Gwynn, Henning, Horus, Kendall, Medea, Meilyr, Merrick, Minos, Oberon, Odin, Paris, Pilan, Rainier, Rane, Regan, Roarke, Rory, Thea, Theodric, Theone, Thierry, Tia, Tibalt, Vanir, Vasilios, Yepa, Zeus

Sadness: Acheron, Airmid, Dido, Iocasta, Jocasta, Rue

Salmon: Malila

Savior: Xavier

Sea: Coral, Maren, Okeanos, Pelagia, Salina, Thalassa, Ula

Serpent: Orinda, Pythia

Sharp: Acacia, Acuzio, Briar, Brier, Motega, Thorne

Shining: Bel, Belenus, Belinus, Dagobert, Delling, Electra, Phedra

Silence: Tacita

Silver: Arian, Ariana, Arianrhod, Arianwen

Skill: Adriel, Arachne, Kai, Lugh, Macon, Meleager, Minerva, Penelope, Sayer, Wapeka

Sleep: Hypnos

Smith: Farrar, Gowan

Son: Brogi, Cuchulainn, Fenrir, Gawain, Gaynor, Galahad, Icarus, Ingmar, Kai, Kei, Kiernan, Madison, Mordred, Modred, Perseus, Yuma

Snow: Chilali, Istas, Malvina

Sorrow: Achall, Acheron, Dido, Igraine, Iocasta, Jocasta, Trista, Tristan, Willow

Spear: Gerald, Gertrude, Jarvis, Osa

Speed: Accursius, Brice, Camilla, Hermes, Iris, Malila, Tabitha

Stranger: Gale, Peregrin

Strength: Achilles, Aindrea, Alectorian, Amber, Andra, Athena, Arnwald, Beowulf, Birkita, Brand, Breasal, Brietta, Brigid, Brigit, Bridgette, Bridget, Brunhilde, Cuchulainn, Elfreda, Fergus, Hagan, Hector, Herakles, Kearney, Leander, Leandra, Magni, Mathilda, Minka, Obelia, Obelix, Ogma, Treasa, Virgil

Sword: Brand, Quillon, Saxon, Zeva

Thunder: Taima, Tama, Terrel, Thor, Thurston, Tora

Trade: Agora, Hermes, Paxton

Travel: Errol, Desmond, Odessa, Peregrin, Quest

Tree: Ackley, Acton, Alaqua, Alder, Ash, Barklay, Birk, Jolon, Laurel, Magnolia, Oakley, Rowan, Thorne, York

Truth: Alathea, Layna, Vera, Verity

Unity: Pietas, Unity

Valley: Camden, Glynis, Hadden, Jolon, Slade

Victory: Kelsey, Nicodemus, Zelinda

War: Aegir, Aer, Aeron, Akando, Akecheta, Alvar, Andraste, Andrasta, Arailt, Ares, Badb, Balor, Bellona, Caelan, Camulos, Camulus, Cayden, Cocidius, Eris, Fianna, Geirolul, Harvey, Hervor, Hrist, Inanna, Ivar, Judur, Kaie, Kera, Kearney, Kellan, Killian, Kincaid, Macha, Madison, Minerva, Niamh, Olrun, Raynor, Tyr, Viveca

Warrior: Achilles, Akecheta, Ares, Athena, Balan, Balin, Balor, Brigid, Brigit, Bridgette, Bridget, Caelan, Camulos, Camulus, Fianna, Inanna, Ivar, Kearney, Kellan, Mathilda, Morgan, Morganna, Moriarty,

Morrigan, Morrigu, Morrighan, Murphy, Odysseus, Olrun, Owen, Patamon, Rathgrith, Reginlief, Rota, Sangridr, Sloan, Thane, Valda, Valkyrie, Zelda

Wealth: Alectorian, Charis, Cresside, Dilys, Eamon, Etania, Freya, Freyja, Freyr

Wild: Blair, Herne, Holda, Sheridon, Thera

Wind: Anemone, Aura, Boreas, Canace, Nodin, Tadi

Wisdom: Achikar, Aglaia, Athena, Badb, Cerridwen, Conner, Connor, Daly, Danu, Druantia, Kendra, Kyna, Mackenzie, Mimir, Minda, Minerva, Odin, Ophelia, Quinn, Ragnar, Ragnhild, Sage, Shannon, Sofi, Sophie, Taliesin

Wolf: Fenrir, Lupercus, Lykaios, Phelan, Randolph, Tala, Ulf, Ulrich, Ilrika, Wolfgang, Wolfram

Woman: Edlyn, Mahala, Orla, Quenby, Vevila

Wrath: Odysseus, Ulysses

Yellow: Xanthe, Xanthus

Fairy/Elven/Dwarven Names: Aeval, Aillil, Aine, Alberich, Alvar, Alwyn, Aylwin, Ariel, Aubrey, Biersal, Blathnat, Caer, Donagh, Elfreda, Ellyllon, Elvin, Etain, Fay, Grian, Kikimora, Luella, Mab, Melusina, Nissa, Nisse, Nixie, Oberon, Pixie, Radella, Roane, Shayla, Tania, Titania, Uldra

Solar names: Apollo, Asa, Aurora, Bel, Belenus, Belinus, Dagna, Dagobert, Dawn, Delling, Dysis, Grian, Helaku, Hemera, Levana, Lucifer, Misae, Mithra, Ra

Lunar names: Aine, Aradia, Artemis, Calisto, Cerridwen, Dana, Dannan, Danu, Diana, Emania, Hecate, Hekate, Isadora, Jacy, Luna, Magena, Miakoda, Migina, Mitena, Mitexi, Neoma, Neona, Nimue, Nokomis, Philomena, Selene, Selina, Tiann, Tayen

Celestial Names: Aither, Amalthea, Andromeda, Arianrhod, Celeste, Juno, Jupiter, Orion, Sidra, Urania

Water Names: Actinia, Adristiea, Aegir, Apsu, Beryl, Boann, Boyne, Brigantia, Brishan, Brooke, Calder, Chumani, Circe, Clota, Coral, Cordelia, Coventina, Danu, Delbin, Dylan, Eudora, Evadne, Huyana, Jasper, Kelda, Kell, Kelvin, Kenn, Kyla, Leith, Malila, Maren, Melia, Meredith, Marla, Marlin, Merla, Merlin, Merrick, Morgan, Morgana, Morganne, Moriarty, Morrigan, Morrigu, Morrighan, Murphy, Naia, Naida, Nairn, Nerissa, Nirvelli, Nixie, Okeanos, Pearl, Pelagia, Poseidon, Proteus, Remus, Salina, Tallulah, Thalassa,

Tiamat, Ula

Earth Names: Abey, Ackley, Acton, Ahearn, Amaethon, Anu, Anann, Ardwinna, Astarte, Blair, Briar, Brier, Brodie, Bryar, Bryn, Calixto, Ceres, Demeter, Enkidu, Fauna, Flidais, Flora, Forrest, Gaea, Gaia, Herne, Kaelyn, Kaia, Landon, Maia, Orrin, Panos, Pembroke, Silva, Silvanus, Slade, Slevin, Talfryn, Terena, Terra, Valonia, Wyome, Xylia, Xylona, Zea

Fire Names: Abomizine, Aed, Aeddon, Aidan, Bel, Belenus, Belinus, Edan, Egan, Ember, Farrar, Gowan, Iagan, Kai, Orinda, Prometheus, Vesta

Air Names: Aeolus, Anemone, Aura, Azure, Bertram, Boreas, Canace, Nodin, Nuit, Tadi, Yakecan, Zephyr

Place Names: Acton, Asgard, Avalon, Barden, Barklay, Bryn, Caerleon, Caerwyn, Carling, Casilda, Erin, Erinn, Eryn, Erynne, Erlina, Glynis, Hadden, Jolon, Kade, Kaelyn, Kelda, Kelvin, Kerr, Kiona, Landon, Leith, Logan, Nairn, Oakley, Olympia, Orrin, Sabrina, Shayla, Tartaros, Valonia, Vance, Whitby, York

Multiple/Sibling Names:

Anu (Anann), Badb, Macha (F)

Apollo (M), Artemis (F) (twins)

Balan, Balin (M)

Banba, Eriu, Fotia (F)
Atropos, Klothos, Lachesis (F)
Freya (Freyja)(F) Freyr (M)
Antigone, Ismene (F)
Tavis, Tevis (M)
Remus, Romulus (M)

Bibliography:

Bulfinch, Thomas. *Bulfinch's Mythology: The Age of Fable.* Garden City, New York: Doubleday & Company, Inc., 1968.

Conway, D.J. *Celtic Magic.* St. Paul, MN: Llewellyn Publications, 1990.

Cunningham, Scott. *Cunningham's Encyclopedia of Crystal, Gem & Metal Magic.* St. Paul, MN: Llewellyn Publications, 1988.

D'aulaire, Ingri & Edgar Parin. *D'aulaire's Book of Greek Myths.* New York: Delacorte Press, 1962.

D'aulaire, Ingri & Edgar Parin. *D'aulaire's Book of Norse Myths.* New York: New York Review of Books, 1995.

Dixon-Kennedy, Mike. *Arthurian Myth & Legend.* London: Brockhampton Press, 1998.

Duane, O.B. *Celtic Myths & Legends.* London: Brockhampton Press, 1998.

Evslin, Bernard. *Gods, Demigods, & Demons: An Encyclopedia of Greek Mythology.* New York: Scholastic Inc., 1975.

Evslin, Bernard & Dorothy, & Hoopes, Ned. *The Greek Gods.* New York: Scholastic, 1966.

Evslin, Bernard & Dorothy, & Hoopes, Ned. *Heroes & Monsters of Greek Myth.* New York: Scholastic, 1967.

Guiley, Rosemary Ellen. *The Encyclopedia of Witches & Witchcraft* (Second edition). New York: Facts on File, Inc., 1999.

Homer. *The Iliad.* 13 Jun. 2012 <http://pd.sparknotes.com/lit/iliad>.

Homer. *The Odyssey.* 13 Jun. 2012 <http://pd.sparknotes.com/lit/odyssey>.

Jones, Allison. *Dictionary of World Folklore.* New York: Larousse, 1995.

Jordon, Michael. *Encyclopedia of Gods: Over 2,500 Deities of the World.* New York: Facts On File, Inc., 1993.

McCoy, Edain. *Making Magick: What It Is and How It Works.* St. Paul, MN: Llewellyn Publications, 1997.

Morford, Mark & Lenardon, Robert. *Classical Mythology* (Fourth edition). New York: Longman, 1991.

Norman, Teresa. *A World Of Baby Names.* New York: Perigree, 1996.

Petras, Kathryn & Ross. *Mythology: Tales & Legends of the Gods.* New York: Workman Publishing, 1998.

Raffel, Burton, trans. *Beowulf*. New York: Mentor, 1963.

Squire, Charles. *Celtic Myth & Legend.* North Hollywood, CA: Newcastle Publishing Co., Inc., 1975.

Printed in Great Britain
by Amazon